the photographer's guide to the California Coast

Where to Find Perfect Shots and How to Take Them

Douglas Steakley

THE COUNTRYMAN PRESS
WOODSTOCK, VERMONT

First Edition

Library of Congress Cataloging-in-Publication Data:
Data has been applied for.

ISBN 0-88150-649-4

Cover and interior photographs by the author
Cover and interior design by Susan Livingston
Maps by Paul Woodward, © The Countryman Press

Published by The Countryman Press, P.O. Box 748, Woodstock, VT 05091
Distributed by W.W. Norton & Company, Inc., 500 Fifth Avenue, New York, NY 10110

Printed in Spain by Artes Graficas Toledo

10 9 8 7 6 5 4 3 2 1

Title page: Bodega Bay headlands
Facing Page: Sunset on Tomales Bay

Dedicated to Jackie and Nicole.
And to Jeri and Michael, who make my
photography possible. . . .

The bluffs at Big Sur

Contents

Introduction

California has a large and diverse coastline, from towering redwood forests in the north to warm and wide surfing beaches in the south. It stretches for 1,100 miles, covers 15 counties, and has numerous national, state, regional, and county parks. In spite of the fact that 90 percent of the coastal wetlands have been destroyed, 97 percent of the old-growth redwoods have been cut for lumber, and almost every river has been dammed, there are still vast stretches of pristine coastal lands with little evidence of human interference. Two examples are the "lost coast" area north of Mendocino and the remote northern shoreline of Santa Barbara County. Plus many wetland areas, estuaries, and marshes, such as Humboldt Bay National Wildlife Reserve and Elkhorn Slough, are teeming with wildlife.

I have visited most of the locations I describe in this book several times and am very familiar with the central coast area around Monterey and Big Sur, where I live. One of the things I enjoy most about being a photographer is the opportunity it provides to visit beautiful areas at the best times: sunrises, sunsets, and during stormy weather. However, I think it would take years of travel to be at the many beaches and streams along the California coastline during different seasons and in different conditions; and most locations vary widely, depending on the time of year, the tides, and the weather. Some beaches look better at low tide, some at high tide, and almost every location looks better in the winter or the spring when grasses are green and wildflowers are blooming. It is

Starfish in a tide pool

my hope that this book will provide a strong overview of many locations that offer good environments for photography. Whenever possible, I have tried to point out the times and conditions that will make for the best photographs.

I have to say something about the difficulty of photographing in southern California, especially in Los Angeles and San Diego Counties. Traffic congestion and development make finding good locations and parking much more difficult than in northern and central California. Probably most of the photographers who live in southern California take trips to more accessible areas when they want to enjoy a few days with their cameras. It has always been a struggle for me to find photogenic locations in southern California due to the difficulty of driving on freeways, where traffic moves at a frustratingly slow pace. As a result I have emphasized or focused more on locations in the northern and central parts of the state.

How I Photograph the California Coast

It's dark, it's cold, and I just turned my windshield wipers on to clear off the mist—or is it rain? It's 4:30 in the morning, and the sun will begin to rise in about an hour. The familiar aroma of freshly brewed coffee fills the car and is somehow comforting. I remind myself that I have done this many times before, and occasionally it works out and I get a great shot. There is a sliver of sky showing beneath the clouds to the east, and if I am lucky, the light from the sun will shine through this crack and illuminate the clouds with a bright pink or orange glow. I am heading for Fisherman's Wharf in Monterey, looking for the light and conditions that occur about once a month and make great photographs. For us photographers this is called "chasing the light," and we all do it. I often get up early and walk out on my deck to check the sky. If it is clear with no clouds, I will go back to bed because I know the sunrise will be beautiful but not spectacular, and I am looking for that magic moment when all the elements of light and subject matter come together. Over the years I have learned that the subject matter is only a small part of a successful photograph and that the lighting on that subject is, by far, the most important ingredient.

There are a variety of good lighting situations, including sunrises and sunsets, foggy or cloudy days, and days with interesting weather like rain, snow, and lightning. I usually steer away from bright, clear days with blue skies—but not always.

I like to photograph in the minutes just before the sun rises, in the late afternoon when the light is warm and horizontal, and just after sunset. The warm light that occurs at these times of day has a large impact on the subject matter, especially with color photography. Rocks that are normally gray or white will turn brown and take on a glow. Lighthouses that are tall, cold white columns are side lit and much warmer and more interesting. When you have the opportunity to photograph in early or late hours, I strongly suggest that you take advantage of it. If there are clouds in the sky that the sun can get under and illuminate, these can become an important element of your photograph and are much more visually interesting than a blank sky.

On days when there is a thin cloud cover and you can barely see your shadow, the colors of your subjects will be much more vivid and saturated than when the sun is out and the sky is clear. If you are visiting a redwood forest or any forest area, your images will be more pleasing on cloudy or overcast days. Fortunately we have a lot of these days during the winter along the California coastline, and during the summer we often have fog, which creates a similar condition. I even like it better if there is a mist in the air or if it has recently rained or is raining. (To protect my equipment, I carry an inexpensive shower cap to place over my camera and lens when I am walking around in the rain or mist.) Don't let wet weather put you off or discourage you—yes, it can be slightly uncomfortable, but the quality of the photographs that you get will be much higher. It takes a rainfall to bring the mosses on redwood trees to life—they "stand up," and the green is much brighter. Actually, water on any subject matter makes the colors more vivid and brighter. You may want to use a polarizer if there is a glare from the wetness, but often I shoot without one. Try it both ways, and see which you prefer with the given conditions.

I don't want to be totally discouraging about photographing during the middle of the day or when the sun is out. There *are* some images you can take under these conditions. Let me think . . . what would those be? Well, if you have a blue sky with puffy white clouds, it is much better than no clouds at all. If the clouds are going to stay around, I would wait until later in the afternoon, or get up early to shoot in the morning. There are many nice landscape shots that can be taken in these conditions, and, of course, if you are traveling, there is not always an alternative. Daytime is also a good time to head for the harbors and photograph the reflections of boats or buildings. I try to find areas where the water is calm but not totally still to photograph reflections. And, yes, the sun is also needed to create rainbows on waterfalls. Look for situations where the sun is behind you as you face the waterfall, and you will often find rainbows in the mist. But as a general rule I use the daylight hours to scout for locations that I can return to when lighting conditions are better.

So what happened on that morning when I got up early to go to Fisherman's Wharf? Well, the photograph is shown below; I was lucky and the conditions were great. I have been to this location many times and only once or twice were clouds and light this cooperative. I have sold this image numerous times to magazines and calendars, so it was certainly worth the effort to get up early to chase the good light.

Sunrise over Fisherman's Wharf

Using This Book

In my workshops I encourage participants to walk around the locations we visit and notice what catches their attention. Different scenes will attract different people and prompt them to look more closely. The suggestions in this book should be taken in the same manner: Here is a good location where you can take your time, walk around and keep your eyes open, notice what you are drawn to, and make this the subject of your images. And when you have found a location or scene that you like, don't take just one photograph; move around the area, and take shots from various angles and heights.

The best photographs are both familiar and fresh; they show us something we have not seen before or a new way of seeing the familiar. Strong images are a discovery for both the photographer and the viewer. And, as with any artistic expression, it takes a bit of courage to create an image that comes from your personal vision.

Manchester State Beach

This book can be used by photographers at any level, from point-and-shoot camera users to advanced amateurs and professionals. But I always have in mind the people who take workshops, seeking to learn more technical information while improving their compositions. I am frequently asked about the locations of photographs I have taken and the right time to be there, so I have tried to include all of this information in the text. Of course, there is always the element of luck—of being in a spot when the light and the weather are just right. But I always remind myself that luck is where opportunity meets preparation.

Photography requires a certain amount of technical and aesthetic knowledge that must be learned and assimilated so that when the moment presents itself, you are prepared. I compare it to learning a language or a musical instrument: Nothing replaces practice, practice, practice. Following is a list of pointers that I frequently review in workshops.

Ten Steps to Help You Improve Your Photography

1. Develop an individual style. Always ask yourself before you shoot: What am I photographing? What attracts me to this scene? After a while you will observe common "threads" in subjects that appeal to you, and as you use these threads in your images over and over, you will develop a personal style. It may take years, but your unique vision will emerge over time.

Several important ingredients go into

making any image successful: lighting, subject matter, and composition, of course, but in the long run the most important ingredient is you, the photographer. As time goes by, the process becomes quicker and easier.

2. Location, location, location. Walk around the subject, or move around the scene, and look through the viewfinder several times before mounting your camera on a tripod. While you are moving around, notice where the light is coming from and how light from different angles changes the image.

It is much easier and faster to improve the composition with the camera in your hands rather than on a tripod. After you have narrowed the options and adjusted the height of the tripod to frame the image, place the camera on the tripod mounting, and look again. This is another way of saying: Slow down and maximize the scene in front of you.

This process of selecting where to shoot an image from has become much easier with the advent of digital cameras. Now it is possible to take several test shots without the tripod and look at them either on the camera's viewing screen or on a laptop. You can always delete these images after you have narrowed down the positions you like the best, and then begin shooting with a tripod.

3. Learn the basic rules or guidelines of composition. Improving the way you compose a photograph will have a large impact on the finished print. Beginning photographers almost always place the subject of the photograph directly in the center of the frame instead of off to one side. We have all seen photographs of people where the heads are in the center

of the image, and the legs are cut off just below the knees. This common mistake is a good example of not being aware of how the image will look on a rectangular "canvas," or print. This same mistake is often made in outdoor scenic photography when the subject of the photograph is placed squarely in the center.

There is a basic rule of composition called the "Rule of Thirds." This means drawing four imaginary lines—two horizontal and two vertical—on the layout of the finished print so that the horizontal and vertical spaces are divided into thirds. These lines will intersect in the upper and lower corners, and it is at one of these four points of intersection where the subject of the photograph should be placed. Off-center placement creates a visual tension in the finished image by making the viewer look both at the subject and the free space where there is no subject or where there can be a second subject. Visually, off-center subjects are much more dynamic and interesting to the viewer.

The same rule applies to the horizon line. Instead of placing the horizon line in the center of the image, either raise or lower it so that the image is divided into thirds rather than halves.

Another basic rule of composition is to have two subjects in the photograph that relate to each other and cause the viewer to look back and forth between them. Even better: Place these so that one is lower than the other instead of being side by side. Upper and lower placement creates an imaginary diagonal line, which creates a visual tension that is more interesting than a horizontal or vertical layout.

Another way to use diagonal lines is by creating "leading lines," or lines that cause the viewer to visually enter the photograph

The Golden Gate Bridge shot from one angle . . .

at one of the corners. For example, if you include a stream or a road in an image, have it begin near the lower left hand corner and lead the viewer's eye into the center or right-hand side where there can be something else that is visually interesting.

When you are photographing, keep these simple guidelines in mind: Move the subject off center, don't split the horizon, and look for lines that lead the viewer's eye into the photograph.

4. Filters can improve many images. It is important to understand how to use the basic filters. The ones that I use most often are a **polarizer,** several **split neutral-density filters,** and an **81A,** or **warming filter.** Numerous other filters are available that produce a wide range of special effects, but I'll focus on these filters, which I use frequently and think are essential.

Photographing along the California coastline—or any scene that includes sky and shore—it is very common to use neutral-density filters. In almost all cases these filters darken the sky to bring it into

the same tonal range as the foreground, producing an image of even tonality instead of a bright (overexposed) sky and a dark (underexposed) foreground. The neutral-density filters I use are flat sheets of plastic that are darkened at one end and left neutral or clear at the other. They come in a variety of strengths such as two stop, three stop, or more and can either be hard or soft edged in the transition area between light and dark. I sometimes use a Cokin holder, which mounts on the end of the lens with an adapter ring that you can buy to fit the millimeter size of the lens. In many situations I do not use the Cokin holder but just carefully hold the neutral-density filter over the end of the lens and adjust it up and down.

With a little practice and understanding, neutral-density filters are easy to use. First, take spot-meter readings off the lighter area in the sky and a second reading off the darker area of the foreground. Often there will be several stops of difference between the two, and without a neutral-density filter, the sky will be too light and the foreground too dark. If there are three stops of difference, I usually use a two-stop neutral-density filter so that the sky will remain somewhat lighter, which is more natural looking. If I am not certain about the difference, or if it is a great shot that I want to be sure I capture, I will often take the same shot with different strengths of neutral density—both a two and a three stop.

As the sky is darkened, the foreground is lightened, which brings out much more information and detail. The goal is to take a photograph of even tonality, avoiding extreme light and extreme dark areas.

Digital cameras offer a real advantage when using neutral-density filters. You can take a couple of test shots with different filters to see how they affect the image, and then select the filter with the correct strength—two stop, three stop, etc. Before I began using a digital camera, I would often shoot several images with different neutral-density filters just to be sure I had the shot. Now I take a picture and evaluate whether or not the neutral-density filter is having the effect I want to achieve.

A polarizer is a very important filter in several situations. First of all a polarizer can remove glare and some haze from an image, so if you are photographing around water or on a wet day, a polarizing filter will eliminate a lot of the reflected light and allow the colors to be more saturated and vibrant. A polarizer can also darken the sky, creating more distinction between it and the clouds. If you have polarized sunglasses, you can see some of the effect of a polarizing filter—but be sure to remove them before you look through the viewfinder when you are using a polarizing filter.

As soon as I get up to about 4,000 feet in the mountains, where the sky is already a deep blue, I usually put my polarizer away. At high altitudes a polarizer will

. . . and from another

A basic guideline of composition is called the "Rule of Thirds," as seen in this image taken at Rocky Point along the Big Sur coastline.

turn the sky dark, and the rich blue will be lost. Remember that a polarizing filter is most effective when used at a 90-degree angle, or perpendicular to the sun, and is not effective shooting either into the sun or with the sun behind your back.

The third filter that I find very useful is an 81A–warming filter that balances or eliminates the bluish/grayish cast in shadow or cloudy areas. For instance, if you are shooting white aspen trees either early or late or on a cloudy day, they sometimes take on a bluish coloration that is neither accurate nor appealing. An 81A will warm up the scene by balancing the blue that tends to show up in these situations. When I use an 81A, I usually shoot the scene with and without the filter, and decide later which image I prefer. If you are using a digital camera, a similar effect can be achieved by adjusting the white balance to "cloudy." You can also add the effect of an 81A in Photoshop and turn it on and off to see which is more appealing. It is a selection under "Adjustments."

Of course, many images turn out better without any filter. For example, when I photograph colorful flowers, I almost never add a filter.

5. "See like a camera." Seeing like a camera means thinking about the separation between objects in a photograph. Remember that the three-dimensional scene you are looking at will be transferred into a flat, two-dimensional image, so make sure that all the subjects have their own space and are not overlapping the subject next to it. For instance, whenever possible, try to separate clouds from trees and trees from each other. Objects that seem far away and invisible will become much more prominent when the image is flattened out and

everything is on one plane. That car in the background may be very small and hard to see, but in the finished print it may be the first thing that catches your eye.

6. Be very careful of the background. This guideline is an extension of the one above. I have noticed in workshops that beginning photographers often pay attention only to their primary subject without realizing that objects in the corners will become very visible in the finished print. Take your time and look in all corners of the viewfinder, not just in the center. Watch for unwanted objects that you are not focusing on but that will appear in the final image, and recompose to avoid these. It is all right to remove any litter and move branches and bright rocks or anything else that will pull the eye from the subject of the photograph. In a way, taking a photograph is like painting: You can selectively add or eliminate items by recomposing or moving them out of the way.

When photographing wildlife, it is often better to let the background be soft or out of focus so long as the subject or animal is sharp. Hand-holding a large telephoto is difficult, and remember the rule of thumb that your shutter speed has to match or exceed your focal length—in other words if you are using a 400mm lens, your shutter speed has to be at least 1/400th of a second or more. Many of the new lenses have VR (vibration reduction), which helps stabilize the image.

7. Be certain that you use the appropriate lens. Perhaps the most important reason to upgrade or purchase a single lens reflex (SLR) camera body is that you can easily change lenses. Changing lenses is not the same as changing position. In other words, shooting with a telephoto

Wildlife photos are often better with the subject in sharp focus and a soft or out-of-focus background.

lens is not the same as walking closer to the subject because as you walk closer, you change the perspective as well as the visual relationship between the objects in the photograph. On the other hand, changing from a wide-angle lens to a telephoto does not alter your perspective; all the elements that you are seeing will remain in your field of vision. Telephoto lenses will eliminate some of these elements because they narrow the range of vision, which allows you to isolate or crop the scene; whereas wide-angle lenses have a wider angle of vision and include more information.

The correct lens selection has to do with how you see or want to record the scene. If you want a broad, sweeping image, a wider angle lens is more appropriate, whereas if you want to isolate or select a smaller area of the scene, a longer or telephoto lens should be used. A telephoto lens will also pull in objects that are in the background, such as mountains, and make them a larger component of the image.

Lenses come in different focal lengths, and focal length refers to the distance between the film plane and the center of the

lens. A wide-angle lens such as a 20mm or 24mm is called a "short lens" because this distance is small, allowing for a wider angle of vision. A telephoto lens, such as a 200mm or 300mm, is often referred to as a "long lens" because the focal length is greater and the angle of vision narrower.

I prefer wide-angle lenses for landscapes because the wide angle of vision includes so much information about the scene. But broad landscapes are not very interesting without something in the foreground being included in the photograph to give it a sense of depth and perspective. With a wide-angle lens such as a 20mm or 24mm, it is possible to include a flower, rock, tree branch, or some other object very close to the lens and have this object and the entire scene remain in sharp focus. With a 20mm lens, an object in the foreground can be as close as 12 inches away. For landscape scenes I often get on my knees to include something in the foreground and then carefully arrange this object in one of the lower corners and compose the background. I prefer my landscape scenes to have foreground, middle ground, and background to provide a sense of perspective so that the viewer feels as though he or she can walk into the scene.

Medium-focal-length lenses such as a 50mm are best suited for intimate scenes that do not emphasize the foreground and background. A good example would be a group of trees or boulders. When I photograph in Yosemite or in the redwoods, I often use a medium-focal-length lens.

Telephoto lenses can be used in a couple of different ways. A long lens can isolate the subject matter such as wildlife or even a flower. A long lens can also make the subject larger within the frame of the photograph. For example, a setting or rising moon will appear much larger in the scene with a 200mm or 300mm lens. If you want to photograph a rising moon and include a tree on the horizon line, stand back from the tree, and use a telephoto to increase the size of the moon and the tree.

In all of these situations it is very important to use a tripod. When I take landscape photographs with a wide-angle lens I always shoot on aperture priority and close the aperture down to f16 or smaller. It is the small aperture opening that allows the entire scene to be in sharp focus. When the aperture is closed down to f16, the shutter speed will be slower, and without a tripod there will certainly be some "camera shake," resulting in an image that is out of focus. A similar problem occurs with telephoto lenses, which are usually too large and heavy to be handheld successfully. Some new lenses have a vibration reduction or internal stabilization feature, which helps when shooting wildlife, but even then the aperture should be open so that the shutter speed is fast.

Lenses work differently on digital SLR (single lens reflex) cameras than on traditional film cameras. With digital cameras, the lenses are more "powerful" than they are on equivalent film cameras. There is approximately a 50 percent increase in the focal length of the lenses because the image sensors on digital cameras are smaller than the size of a negative or transparency in film cameras. Accordingly, a 20mm lens becomes a 30mm and a 400mm lens becomes a 600mm. As a result, the first lens I had to purchase for my digital body was a 12–24mm wide-angle zoom lens because the 20mm lens that I used for my film camera was no longer wide enough for the landscapes I like to shoot.

8. Learn the basic principles of correct exposure. It is a common mistake to think that the sophisticated light meters in today's cameras will give correctly exposed photographs every time you take a picture. The most important thing to bear in mind about camera light meters is that they will render your image in a middle tone, and not all scenes are middle tone. Middle tone means that light areas such as snow or clouds will be made darker, and black areas such as shadows will be made lighter. This may not matter if snow or shadows are a small portion of the photograph since the light meter will average out the various tonalities, but it will matter a lot if light or dark areas make up a large portion of the image. For instance, if you are shooting a scene where a sky with white puffy clouds takes up more than half of the image, the light meter will darken the clouds and also darken the foreground or lower half of the photograph so that a lot of the image will be dark, or underexposed. Although this principle affects all types of film and digital cameras, it is particularly true with transparency or slide film.

Different lenses allow for different angles of vision

Most modern cameras have a spot meter, which allows you to measure reflected light by aiming the center of your viewfinder at an object or a portion of a scene and taking a light reading from that limited area. Look for something in the scene that is a middle tone or something in the scene that you want to have exposed as middle tone. Tree trunks, green grass, gray boulders, the blue sky are usually middle tone, so you can point your spot meter at them and take a reading. Then switch your camera to manual mode, and dial in these settings, or leave it on aperture priority and adjust the exposure compensation to reach the settings you had with the spot meter.

Here's how it works: I usually shoot in aperture priority and often at f11 or f16, so I will set my camera in aperture prior-ity mode at f16 and take a spot reading off something in the scene that I want to have exposed in middle tonality. This might give me a reading of f16 at 1/15th of a second. I then turn my camera to manual mode at these settings, or I leave it in aperture priority, return the meter to matrix reading, and then adjust the exposure compensation until I have the setting I am looking for. From there I usually bracket up and down in small increments by changing the exposure compensation.

Recently I was photographing a scene in Yosemite with a lot of snow, and I knew that if I relied on the matrix reading, it would darken the snow. So I took a spot reading off a nearby tree trunk, then adjusted my exposure compensation. In this case I increased my exposure time by 1.5 stops. If there is a lot of snow and the

Learn the basic principles of correct exposure

scene is very white, the exposure compensation may be plus 2. With this amount of compensation, the scene is being overexposed enough to allow the snow to remain white.

Images that are always difficult to meter are sunsets or sunrises, winter scenes, waterfalls, dark or light animals or flowers, and any backlit scenes. Take your time and think about what portion of the image you want to have rendered as middle tone. I usually bracket my images by about .3 to .7 of a stop either way with transparency film or with my digital camera. Sometimes an over- or underexposed image has more visual impact than an image exposed as middle tone.

These same principles apply to digital cameras. Don't fall into the trap of thinking that you can correct all of your digital images in Photoshop. A correctly exposed photograph is much easier to work with, whether shot with film or shot digitally. One big advantage of using digital cameras is that you can get instant feedback in difficult situations. I often find that I increase or decrease my exposure compensation in small increments while taking a series of shots and delete the ones that are obviously too dark or too light.

9. Shoot both vertical and horizontal formats of the same scene. This is especially true if you plan to sell your images. I often receive requests for vertical images for magazine covers, whereas some calendars accept only horizontal images. If you are shooting an image that you think might be appropriate for a magazine cover, be certain to leave a blank area at the top—such as blue sky—where the title of the magazine can be printed. The most difficult part of photography is being in

Door knocker at Fort Ross
State Historic Park

the right place at the right time, so while you are there, you should maximize your efforts by remembering to shoot the scene both ways.

10. Remember that you are creating a personal image, not just recording the scene in front of you. Perhaps more than any other art form, photography has the power to enable us to "see" an image in a way that we have never seen it before. As photographers we select a portion or elements in a scene that are important to us and include them in the photograph. When this is done well, photographs record and present the familiar with a directness that often takes the viewer by surprise. You can focus on any subject matter that interests you and then share your personal vision with others. Photography is a form of silent communication that hopefully strikes an emotional cord with those who view your images.

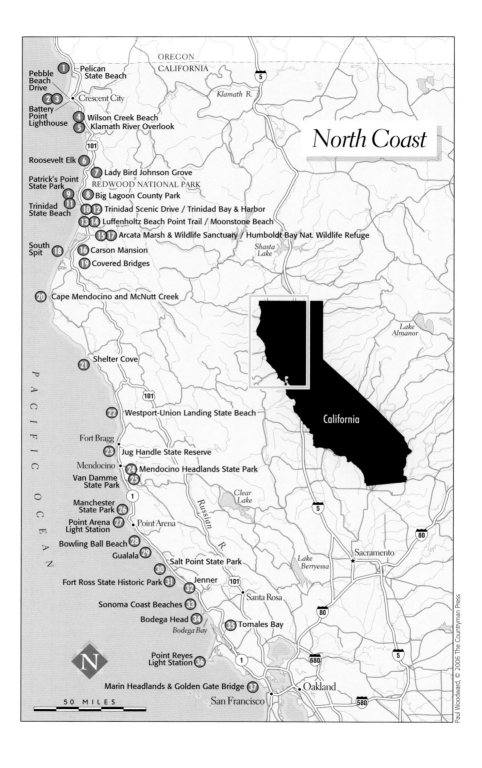

North Coast

OREGON
CALIFORNIA

Klamath R.

1 Pelican State Beach

Pebble Beach Drive
2 3 Crescent City
Battery Point Lighthouse
4 Wilson Creek Beach
5 Klamath River Overlook

101

6 Roosevelt Elk
7 Lady Bird Johnson Grove
Patrick's Point State Park
REDWOOD NATIONAL PARK
9 8 Big Lagoon County Park
11
Trinidad State Beach
10 12 Trinidad Scenic Drive / Trinidad Bay & Harbor
13 14 Luffenholtz Beach Point Trail / Moonstone Beach
15 17 Arcata Marsh & Wildlife Sanctuary / Humboldt Bay Nat. Wildlife Refuge
South Spit 18 16 Carson Mansion
19 Covered Bridges

Shasta Lake

20 Cape Mendocino and McNutt Creek

Lake Almanor

21 Shelter Cove

California

101

22 Westport-Union Landing State Beach

Fort Bragg
23 Jug Handle State Reserve
Mendocino
24 Mendocino Headlands State Park
25
Van Damme State Park
1
Manchester State Park 26
Point Arena Light Station 27 Point Arena
Bowling Ball Beach 28
Gualala 29

Clear Lake

Russian R.

Lake Berryessa

Sacramento

5

80

30 Salt Point State Park
Fort Ross State Historic Park 31 Jenner
32
Sonoma Coast Beaches 33
Bodega Head 34
Bodega Bay
35 Tomales Bay

101
Santa Rosa

80

Point Reyes Light Station 36

1

680

5

N

Marin Headlands & Golden Gate Bridge 37 Oakland
San Francisco

580

50 MILES

PACIFIC OCEAN

Paul Woodward, © 2006 The Countryman Press

North Coast—Oregon to San Francisco

Pelican State Beach (1)

Pelican State Beach, a small beach located just below the Oregon border, marks the beginning of California's 1,100-mile coastline. The park is not very well marked from Highway 101, but you can take the turnoff for Pelican Bay State Penitentiary, across from the Pelican Beach Motel. Driving south, it is just after the state agricultural inspection station. This small beach is littered with driftwood, as are all the beaches in northern California, but Pelican Beach also has very nice grasses that provide a strong foreground for photographs with the beach and rocky shoreline in the background. The best time to photograph along this beach is late afternoon or evening to get cross lighting or on cloudy or foggy days.

Pebble Beach Drive in Crescent City (2)

Pebble Beach Drive is about a 2-mile-long road that runs north from Crescent City along the Pacific Ocean. It starts out in a residential neighborhood and soon changes into a more remote and scenic area. There are many parking areas to pull into, and it is a great place to watch the sun set. There are large sea stacks—offshore isolated blocks of erosion-resistant rock that were once part of a headland or cliff. Some are large enough to support vegetation. A small stream, Marhoffer Creek, runs across the sand into the ocean and is generally full of seagulls. This stream provides a nice leading line into the ocean and the sea stacks. At this beach the early-morning light is good, as are the sunsets. The early light illuminates the sea stacks so that their details are more visible. I suggest that you leave enough time to drive up and down Pebble Beach Drive to find your own favorite place and then return in plenty of time to capture the sunset or early-morning light.

Directions: Driving south on Highway 101, turn west on Washington Boulevard, which dead ends at the northern end of Pebble Beach Drive. Driving north on Highway 101, turn west on Ninth Street, follow it until it dead ends into Pebble Beach, and then turn north.

Battery Point (Crescent City) Lighthouse (3)

This lighthouse is built on a large rocky mound and is very picturesque, especially at sunset. The lighthouse was built in 1855 and became operational in 1856. Built in a Cape Cod style, the lighthouse has its tower located in the center of the residence dwelling. After several families lived in the lighthouse as keepers, it was automated in 1953 and soon became a museum. Today the light remains on at night as an aid to private navigation. Over the years the lighthouse has been hit by several large storms, but surprisingly the large tsunami that hit the area in 1964 did little damage to the lighthouse, even though the 16-foot-high waves destroyed

Battery Point Lighthouse at sunset

many boats in the harbor and the city's central business district.

Directions: From Highway 101 take the Front Street exit, Crescent City, and drive west for 12 blocks until it ends at A Street. Turn left, and drive into the parking lot a couple of blocks down, immediately across from the lighthouse.

Wilson Creek Beach (4)

There are many beach turnouts along Highway 101 between Crescent City and Klamath. I stopped at Wilson Creek because I always look for streams or creeks flowing into the ocean. This small turnout immediately south of the Wilson Creek Bridge is only marked as a county turnout, but it is well worth the visit. The black-sand beach has many large pieces of driftwood that make sculptural forms to include in your images. Closer to where

Wilson Creek flows into the ocean, I found lots of birds and some interesting bird tracks in the wet sand, which made interesting lines leading into photographs of the rugged shoreline and sea stacks to the north. The best light is late afternoon or a cloudy-foggy day, which adds a sense of mystery and interest to your images.

Requa Turnoff to Klamath River Overlook (5)

Requa Turnoff offers dramatic views of the Klamath River to the south and the coastline in both directions. As well as providing picnic tables, this turnoff is also a trailhead for the Coastal Trail, which hugs the cliffs to Lagoon Creek about 1 mile north. I tried to include some of the grasses and bushes in the foreground of my photographs of the Klamath River to give them more dimension and interest. The Klamath River estuary forms a large sandy beach below the parking lot. I was there in the afternoon but would have preferred the evening or early morning, when there would be more of a cross light.

Directions: Follow the signs on Highway 101, which take you 1.5 miles west on Patrick Murphy Memorial Drive to the parking lot for the overlook.

Roosevelt Elk (6)

The largest subspecies of North American elk, Roosevelt elk can often be seen along the Newton B. Drury Parkway in Prairie Creek Redwoods State Park just 6 miles north of Orick. Elk can also be found south of Elk Prairie, just off Highway 101 along Davidson Road. Elk travel in herds, so if you see one, you will almost certainly see more. Although these elk are quite used to having their picture taken, they are wild animals, and the large males can become quite aggressive, especially during fall mating season. Male elk with their large antlers are often seen in the late summer, and the young are born in April and May. My favorite place for photographing elk is along Bald Hills Road, a half mile north of Orick off of Highway 101. This is a narrow road and not recommended for large vehicles or trailers. After you turn onto Bald Hills Road, drive for about 8 miles to an open meadow with oaks and large redwoods in the background.

If you stop at one of the visitors centers, located at both the south and north ends of the Redwood National and State Parks, the very helpful rangers will give you a map and tell you where you are likely to see elk during your trip.

I use my largest telephoto lens (a 400mm) on a tripod with shutter priority

Wilson Creek Beach in northern California

set to 1/250 or more and focus on the animal's eyes. I loosen the ball head so that I can move it fairly easily but keep it tight enough to stop camera shake.

Lady Bird Johnson Grove in Redwood National Park (7)

The Redwood National and State Parks along Highway 101 are a World Heritage Site and an International Biosphere Reserve, to protect the 3 percent of the remaining old-growth redwoods. The drive through the redwoods is always inspiring and beautiful. There are many areas to stop and photograph the redwoods, from the Jedediah Smith Redwoods State Park to the north to the Humboldt Redwoods State Park to the south. I selected the Lady Bird Johnson Grove because it has a 1-mile, 1-hour loop trail that leads through mature forests to the site that Lady Bird Johnson dedicated in 1968.

I have read that the redwoods are the oldest living things in the world, but I have read the same thing about the bristlecone pines that are located east of Bishop, California. The redwoods live up to 1,500 years and grow to heights of 350 feet, taller than the Statue of Liberty. The large redwoods became the second gold rush in California, and in the latter part of the 19th century large areas of the native forests were cut for timber. Fortunately several state parks were formed in the 1920s to preserve some remaining stands of the redwood forests, and in 1968 Redwood National Park was formed, which encircles the three existing state parks and gives increased protection to the ancient redwood forests.

There are many ways to photograph the redwoods, all tricky and requiring care. It is difficult to show the size or scale of the trees without a person or object in the foreground to give a sense of perspective, but I prefer my nature photographs without people. Also, it is often very dark in the redwood groves, but I find more photographs on dark or foggy days, compared to bright sunny skies that usually result in images with too much contrast. I look for trees that are in groups and shoot both vertically and horizontally. Vertical images often add to the drama of the tall trees. I also look for trees that have some color—many of the redwoods have shades of green or yellow in their bark or moss

Lady Bird Johnson Grove in Redwood National Park

Big Lagoon is an important winter flyway

growing on them, rendering them much more interesting than the gray color you often see. I recommend taking your time and shooting a lot of photographs; you can always edit and select the best images later. If you include the sky in your image, be sure to take a reading off the tree bark or the trees will become silhouettes without much detail.

Tip: In April and May the rhododendrons are in bloom and provide a nice contrast to the dark color of the redwoods.

Directions: Turn off Highway 101 onto Bald Hills Road, and follow the curves for about 2 miles. The grove is clearly marked and has a large parking lot and rest rooms. This road is not suitable for trailers or motor homes.

Big Lagoon County Park (8)

Big Lagoon County Park is located 9 miles south of Orick along Highway 101. Here you'll find a large barrier beach and brackish lagoon plus several nice stands of grasses and sedges where creeks flow into the lagoon. I always look for these grasses to use in the foregrounds of my photographs to give them depth and a focal point. In winter Big Lagoon is also an important flyway for many migrating birds.

Patrick's Point State Park (9)

Patrick's Point provides a high overview of the coastline in both directions, with many sea stacks in the background. These rocky crags provide important breeding grounds for many types of birds, sea lions, and seals because they are protected from the many mainland predators. I have not spent much time at this park, but there is much to explore. The Rim Trail, an old Indian trail, goes along the high bluffs and affords views to Trinidad Harbor to the south and Big Lagoon to the north. This is also a good place to observe

Sea stack at Trinidad State Beach

the migrating gray whales in the winter and spring.

Trinidad Scenic Drive (10)

Trinidad Scenic Drive is a small, sometimes one-lane, road that parallels Highway 101 but is closer to the Pacific. From the north, take the Trinidad exit; from the south, take the Westhaven exit. Trinidad Scenic Drive has several excellent places to pull off and photograph the large sea stacks lying offshore several beaches. The most significant of these beaches is Luffenholtz Beach County Park.

Trinidad State Beach (11)

A short, steep trail leads down from the parking lot to Trinidad State Beach, and many other trails go through the redwoods and along a cliff high above the beach. The seascape from the beach is in-

teresting and varied, with small sea stacks in the cove. Mill Creek flows through the beach and can provide a leading line into the photograph with the sea stacks in the background. This is also a good beach for locating and photographing wildlife, especially the large common murres and black oystercatchers that inhabit the rocks offshore. As you walk along the beach, you will also find tide pools, which I always enjoy photographing at low tide. An unpaved parking lot off Stagecoach Road has a trail leading to the headlands and down to College Cove, a charming sandy beach area.

Tip: Take care with the slippery moss-covered rocks that are exposed during low tide. Sometimes it is better to just let your shoes get wet and wade among the rocks instead of trying to step from rock to rock to stay dry.

Directions: Trinidad State Beach is located off Trinity Street, which is north of Main Street in Trinidad. Trinity Street runs parallel to Highway 101, just to the west.

Trinidad Bay and Harbor (12)

The small town of Trinidad, located just west of Highway 101, is a charming combination of a fishing village and summer tourist destination. The quiet streets invite you to park your car and walk to visit the shops and restaurants. Fishing boats dot the harbor, which is spread out below the town, and the local fishermen and their boats make attractive images. In the winter months the local fishermen bring in lots of Dungeness crabs, and I was able to walk out on the pier and get some close-up images of them unloading baskets of crabs. Trinidad and Mendocino are my favorite small towns along the northern California coast; both have dramatic and accessible shorelines, and the towns have interesting streets and shops to explore.

Directions: As you drive south on Highway 101, exit onto Stagecoach Road, which parallels Highway 101 but is closer to the coastline. After about 1.5 miles Stagecoach Road becomes Trinity Street as it enters the small town of Trinidad. I prefer to drive along Stagecoach Road and Trinidad Scenic Drive along this section of the coastline instead of the larger Highway 101.

Luffenholtz Beach Point Trail (13)

The Point Trail at Luffenholtz Beach is a short walk that offers views both north and south of the sea stacks in the Pacific. You can follow the small trail around the point to find better vantage points to photograph up and down the coast. There is also a turnoff for a county fishing access, but this is not the same as the elevated Point Trail.

Directions: To reach Luffenholtz Beach, turn south off of Main Street in Trinidad onto Trinidad Scenic Drive, just west of Highway 101. Luffenholtz Beach is in the middle of the Scenic Drive loop.

Moonstone Beach (14)

This broad, sandy beach is located near the Luffenholtz Beach County Fishing Access and is named for the rounded rocks that have been shaped by the action of the tides and waves. The beach itself has a small, rocky stream and very interesting rock formations. I again used the stream as an image to lead into the scene. The rocks are often covered in a mist, which gives them an ethereal or mysterious feeling. Take your time and compose carefully because there usually is not very much color, and the scenes become black and white—stark and direct. As you come down the trail and cross the stream, look for cave formations in the rocks to the right, which provide some very interesting photo opportunities. Walk about 100 yards, and you will find a fairly large cave formed in the rocks, which you can walk into.

Tip: Shooting from inside the cave out to the beach and ocean can provide an interesting frame to your photographs. The cave walls will turn black and provide an inverted V shape, which can be very dramatic.

Directions: Moonstone Beach is at the southern end of Scenic Drive, 3 miles south of Trinidad.

Arcata Marsh and Wildlife Sanctuary (15)

The Arcata Marsh was created in 1979 by the city of Arcata in an attempt to restore some of the degraded marshland along the north shore of Arcata Bay. A network of trails allows for hiking, bird-watching, and photography. The marsh attracts many species of birds, including egrets and herons, which always make great subjects for photography. There are also some interesting still-life types of photographs here where you can include grasses in the foreground and old, weathered pilings in the water in the background.

Arcata Bay is also an excellent location for photographing the rising sun or moon since you can drive around to the west side of the bay and face east. There are several turnout areas along Highway 255, which is also New Navy Base Road. My favorite locations are just north of the bridge, which crosses to Samoa. You can park and walk a very short distance to the water's edge and get excellent reflections of the sun or moon rising in Arcata Bay.

Tip: I usually use a two- to three-stop neutral-density filter to bring out the foreground when I am photographing reflections in the water that include the sky. The image in the water will always be a little darker as the water absorbs light and color.

Directions: From Highway 101, turn west on Highway 255, and then take a left onto I Street. Signs direct you to the marsh and sanctuary area. To photograph the rising sun or moon, continue around on Highway 255 for about 2 miles until

Sea stacks off Luffenholtz Park Point

you find a pullout area on the western shore of Arcata Bay.

Eureka

Just south of Arcata, Eureka is the largest coastal city in California north of San Francisco. Both Eureka and Arcata became established during the middle of the 19th century as a result of the gold rush in the Trinity region. Early on Arcata was the more important of the two cities because it was situated closer to the gold rush areas, but as the importance of gold declined and the lumber industry prospered, Eureka became the more important of the two cities due to its deepwater harbor. In 1856 the county seat was moved south from Arcata to Eureka, where it has remained. In just a few years' time, seven lumber mills opened in Eureka, and soon there were over 100 schooners in Humboldt Bay transporting lumber to the many cities being built up and down the Pacific coastline. Today Eureka also supports a large commercial fishing fleet and is the entry point for petroleum for this area.

Humboldt Bay, the Eureka Slough, and the Samoa Dunes Recreation Area all provide interesting places for photography, but I prefer the South Bay and South Spit and Elk River areas, which are located south of town.

Carson Mansion (16)

It took master craftsmen two years—from 1884 to 1886—to build lumber baron William Carson's mansion. This very ornate Victorian structure is well worth the side trip to view and photograph. In fact, the Carson Mansion is often touted as the most photographed residence in America. Unfortunately the mansion is now a private club, so it is not possible to see the inside, but the outside is very impressive. A broad porch along the front and south sides of the house provides the two major entrances. Large ornamented pillars rest on top of balusters, which help make the building much more decorative and eye-catching than the other beautiful Victorians in Eureka.

Directions: Driving south on 101, turn west (right) onto M Street, and go about two blocks. The large green mansion will be on the right-hand side at Second Street. In this part of town Highway 101 is a divided street, so if you are driving north, you will have to make a left onto M Street and cross 101 south.

Humboldt Bay National Wildlife Refuge (17)

The Humboldt Bay National Wildlife Refuge protects 8,600 acres of marshes, mud flats, canals, and grassy areas. This large and important refuge provides a fly-over area for many migrating birds, including tundra swans, which can often be seen in large and small groups. There are many other birds, including great egrets and large blue herons. Harbor seals use the mudflats for hauling out and pupping in the spring.

There is access for nonmotorized water craft such as canoes and kayaks, which can get you much closer to the birds for photography. The entire refuge area provides many opportunities to photograph various types of wildlife, from crabs along the shoreline to deer in the marsh grasses. The water level changes dramatically with the tides, so it is prudent to consult a tide table. The ideal time to photograph this area would be during a low tide, which

Tundra swans in Humboldt Bay

attracts egrets, herons, and many shore-birds, at either sunrise or sunset, when the light is softer and more dramatic. This area reminds me of Elkhorn Slough far-ther to the south near Monterey.

Directions: Take the Hookton Road exit off Highway 101 south of Eureka, and fol-low the signs to one of two parking areas. One parking lot is located to the north along Redwood Highway; the other is on the south side of the bay along Hookton Road.

South Spit (18)

The South Spit is a long jetty road head-ing north that separates the southern por-tion of Humboldt Bay from the Pacific Ocean. A long, rugged beach and coast-line offer some photographic possibili-ties, particularly at sunset or sunrise. At sunrise or moonrise you can face east and get reflections on the South Bay.

I was attracted to the large clumps of European beach grasses growing on the dunes. The grasses are unusual in that they grow in isolated clumps and are very interesting visually. Unfortunately, like many interesting plants in California, these grasses are not native and are harm-ful to the native dune habitat.

Directions: The South Spit is just a con-tinuation of Hookton Road, which turns into Table Bluff Road and then South Jetty Road.

Covered Bridges (19)

The two old bridges—which are very sim-ilar and look as though they were built at the same time—provide access over the Elk River and are the westernmost cov-ered bridges in the United States. These bridges are wonderfully photogenic, with very well-maintained weathered wood siding and wooden shingles and green fields on either side. Try to find an angle that eliminates the nearby telephone poles and highway signs to make the bridges look more authentic.

Directions: From Highway 101 south of Arcata, take the Herrick Road/Elk River exit, and follow Elk River Road for about 1 mile and then turn right on Berta Road. The first covered bridge is about 1 mile down Berta Road on the right; the second bridge is the next right-hand turn.

Cape Mendocino and McNutt Creek on Mattole Road (20)

This is a very remote area of California that sees few visitors. Cape Mendocino, the westernmost point in California, is reached by exiting Highway 101 at Ferndale—a well-marked exit just south of Eureka—and following a small, winding country road south about 20 miles. The drive along this very remote road is beautiful, beginning in a forested area, then reaching expansive green, hilly pastures used for cattle grazing. Matolle Road then heads down to the ocean and turns south for several miles, following dunes, beaches, and tide pools. Much of this area is private property, but there are some paths leading to the beaches. (A lighthouse that used to be at Cape Mendocino has been relocated to Shelter Cove, about 25 miles to the south.)

I stopped along this road several times to photograph the rolling hills and small streams. My favorite location was a very small creek called McNutt Creek, located just as the road turns inland and starts to climb away from the ocean. This stream is fenced and on private property, but I was able to stand on the shoulder of the road and take several very nice photographs of the creek with dunes and grasses in the foreground.

It is possible to follow Mattole Road back to Highway 101, or you can turn south on Wilder Ridge Road and drive through the King Range National Conservation Area down to Shelter Cove. If you are low on gas, I recommend driving back out to Highway 101 before turning back to Shelter Cove as gas stations are few and far between in this remote area.

Shelter Cove (21)

Shelter Cove is about a 45-minute drive west off of Highway 101 on a series of narrow winding roads that go through King Range National Conservation Area and some nice stands of redwood groves. I am not sure that Shelter Cove is worth the long trip for photography unless you want to see the relocated Cape Mendocino Lighthouse, which is very similar to the one at Point Reyes. However, Shelter Cove is a popular residential community in the summer and has a couple of nice beaches and tide pools.

The Cape Mendocino Lighthouse was automated in 1951, and the lens was taken to Ferndale, where it remains on display. The lighthouse was totally abandoned in

One of two westernmost covered bridges in the U.S.

1970 and in 1998 disassembled and relocated down the coast in Shelter Cove. The restored lighthouse is now located on a grassy knoll in Mal Coombs Park on a bluff overlooking the Pacific.

Highway 1 North of Fort Bragg: Westport–Union Landing State Beach (22)

Westport–Union Landing State Beach is located about 1.5 miles north of Westport off Highway 1. This beach, like almost all the beaches along this northern coastline,

Westport–Union Landing State Beach from the bluffs

was the site of a schooner landing area, where steam-powered sailing ships could be loaded with freshly cut redwood trees. I found some interesting areas to photograph along the stream, which has a sandy beach on one side and a rocky, hilly shoreline on the other. I prefer these beach areas on foggy, misty days, which fortunately occur frequently in this region.

Jug Handle State Reserve and Pygmy Forest (23)

Jug Handle State Reserve has a large ocean frontage with a beach below the bridge on Highway 1 as well as pines and redwood forests, but it is best known as the location for the Pygmy Forest.

The Pygmy Forest is located at the top of several terraces, which were formed by wave action during the Pleistocene era when the level of the sea rose and fell. The terraces were lifted up by the shifting earth, and sand was deposited on top of the soil. The sandy soil drains off most of the nutrients and the Mendocino cypresses and Bishop and Bolander pines grow to a height of only 5 to 10 feet in the acidic soil. I found it very hard to photograph the stunted trees because it was difficult to show the size of the small trees. I had the most success when I included the raised walkway that winds through the grove because it helped show how small the trees were. Even though this is a frustrating area to photograph, I found the dwarf forest interesting and worth the hike. I also found some very colorful red mushrooms, called "the Sickener" *(Russula emetica)*, along the trail.

Directions: Turn off Highway 1 into Jug Handle State Reserve, which is about a mile north of Mendocino. Once in the park there is a 2.5-mile trail to the Pygmy

Boardwalk in Jug Handle State Reserve

Forest. If you are short of time and want to go more directly to Pygmy Forest, here is a shortcut: Leave the Jug Handle State Reserve, drive north for about 0.5 mile, and turn right on Gibney Lane. Gibney Lane takes a turn to the right; follow it for 0.9 mile to the Old Caspar Railroad Road on your left. There is a turnout on the right-hand side and a small sign noting the state park boundary and a trailhead. Follow this trail under the power lines for about 100 yards until it intersects the main trail. Turn left and continue to the Pygmy Forest, which should take about 20 to 30 minutes from this point. This shortcut reduces the walking time by about half.

Mendocino and Mendocino Headlands State Park (24)

The small town of Mendocino is well known as a tourist destination along California's northern coast. It is also well known for its quaint architecture and many charming bed & breakfasts, small inns, interesting shops and galleries, and excellent restaurants. I prefer to visit Mendocino in the winter months, when the air is often crystal clear and the sun is warmer, than in the summer, when it is often foggy. Mendocino is surrounded by nine state parks with a variety of both inland and beach trails to explore. Many locations in and around Mendocino offer photographic opportunities, from the architecture in the town to the natural environments of the parks. One of my favorite locations is Mendocino Headlands State Park, located a short walk just west of the town. The 2 miles of trails along the high bluffs above the Pacific offer many opportunities for photography. There are large offshore islands, blow holes, a rugged coastline, tide pools, and a sandy beach.

I am particularly intrigued by the large waves, which often crash against the sea stacks and surge through the many tunnels formed in the rocks below by wave action. As when photographing all of California's coastline, the best time to shoot is early morning or sunset.

The "lost coast" of Mendocino: Seal Rock

Note that when photographing the ocean from these high bluffs, you'll often find a strong wind blowing off the water. This wind can pick up a salty mist that can cloud your lenses and cover your camera. It is very important to clean your camera frequently when photographing along the coastline. I use a soft, damp cotton cloth or chamois to wipe off the accumulated salt and moisture. I also wipe off my tripod legs so that they operate more smoothly.

Tip: If conditions are very wet, or if there is a slight rain, I cover my camera and lens with a disposable plastic shower cap. These lightweight caps are available in drug stores and make an excellent cover due to the elastic band around the bottom. I always keep several in my camera bag.

Directions: This state park is located on a marine terrace at the west end of Men-docino. Drive through the town on Ukiah Street, and keep going west until you reach the park.

Van Damme State Park: Fern Canyon Trail (25)

Fern Canyon Trail follows an old logging skid road and the Little River. There are numerous opportunities along this trail to photograph the lush, damp environment, with many ferns, small waterfalls, and quiet pools.

I prefer to use a wide-angle lens in these situations and get very close to the subject. The advantage of wide-angle lenses is that they allow everything in the image to be in sharp focus. Remember that a 20mm lens can focus on a flower or plant less than a foot away in the foreground and still have everything in the background remain in sharp focus.

At the end of the trail you can hike farther to a different Pygmy Forest than the one in Jug Handle State Reserve. This Pygmy Forest is also accessible a little farther south along Highway 1. Follow Highway 1 south, beyond Van Damme State Park, and turn left onto Little River Airport Road. You can park off of Little River Airport Road where it intersects Albion Little River Road, and follow the signs for the trails.

Directions: Van Damme State Park is located 1.3 miles south of Mendocino. The Fern Canyon Trail is east of the highway.

Manchester State Beach (26)

Manchester State Beach—part of Manchester State Park—is different from the beaches farther north in that it does not have large sea stacks or sizeable waves. It is a much calmer environment, with pathways that lead through dunes down to a large, flat, sandy beach. My favorite location is found by leaving the main parking lot and crossing the dunes to a bluff overlooking Brush Creek. Brush Creek flows parallel to the beach and then turns and flows into the ocean, providing a point of focus or leading line to include in photographs. There are nice grasses growing in the dunes that I include in the foreground. From some locations the Point Arena Lighthouse can be seen in the distance.

I enjoy these types of landscapes because I can incorporate several different points of focus and compose them so that they relate to each other visually. I try to find a diagonal line running between two or three focal points because diagonals create a feeling of tension, which can draw the viewer into the image much more than

horizontal and vertical lines. I use a wide-angle lens and often set my tripod very low so that the camera body is very close to some visual point (grasses, a rock) in the foreground. If this foreground is dark, it can be lightened with a gold or white reflector or a handheld flash. Sometimes it is visually interesting to have a lighter object in the foreground since this will draw the viewer's eye into the scene.

Directions: Manchester State Beach is 1 mile north of Manchester and is reached by turning off of Highway 1 onto Kinney Road. There are campsites and a parking lot in the dunes near the beach.

Point Arena Lighthouse (27)

This striking lighthouse is best photographed in late afternoon, when it is lit from the side. I have found it is good to park just outside the entrance gate, then walk across to the bluff on the ocean side, where I can get a good shot of the lighthouse with the eroded cliffs and ocean waves in the foreground. Be sure that your lens is level so that the lighthouse is not leaning in the frame. A couple of guidelines: Remember the rule of thirds, and keep the lighthouse out of the center of the composition, plus try not to split the horizon. The best image, therefore, is where the lighthouse is off to the lower-right side of the frame, and the bluffs in the foreground take up either one-third or two-thirds of the scene, depending on how good the clouds are on the day you visit.

This lighthouse is also very interesting to visit. It still has the original 6-foot-wide Fresnel lens, and there are three lighthouse keeper's cottages available for rent. For more information, call 707-882-2777.

Sunset over the Gualala River

Directions: The turnoff for Point Arena Lighthouse is clearly marked on Highway 1, about 2 miles north of the town of Point Arena. The drive up to the lighthouse goes along the dramatic Point Arena Headlands, where the Garcia River flows into the Pacific.

Bowling Ball Beach (28)

Just 3.5 miles south of Point Arena on Highway 1, Bowling Ball Beach is very interesting to photograph, especially if you can arrive at low tide. These large rocks, called concretions, were formed years ago in the Miocene age and eventually fell onto the beach as the bluff above eroded away. The rocks are very large—6 to 12 feet in diameter—and create dramatic images with the Pacific in the background. There is no sign on Highway 1, but look for the turnout across from Schooner Gulch Road. You can park here, and follow the trail down to the beach.

Gualala (29)

I have driven through Gualala many times and have never stopped to photograph in this area; but recently I was there at sunset and found a pullout at the south end of town that overlooked the mouth of the Gualala River with the Pacific in the background. The river added a strong horizontal element to my compositions, and I was very pleased with the images I was able to take that evening, as shown above.

Salt Point State Park: Gerstle Cove (30)

Salt Point State Park is a clearly marked turnoff of Highway 1 and Gerstle Cove is located within Salt Point State Park. Drive to the end of the road and walk down to the rocky beach. Gerstle Cove is an ecological reserve and an interesting habitat. I like to photograph the abstract and colorful patterns that are formed in the sandstone rock formations, which have been eroded by the ocean waves and wind. These interesting formations remind me of those found at Weston Beach in Point Lobos State Park south of Monterey.

Also, the waves crashing against the sea stacks close to shore put on a dramatic show and make for great images. Some of the larger waves create a spray several times higher than the rocks they are striking. I set my camera up on a tripod with a fairly fast shutter speed, such as 1/125 or 1/60, and wait for the waves to splash—then I take several images in quick succession. The depth of field is not as important in this type of shot as it is in other landscape scenes.

Tip: If you are photographing the patterns on the rock, be sure that the film plane of your camera is parallel to the area you are photographing. This guideline applies to all situations where you are using a macro lens and getting close to the subject. If the camera is not parallel to the subject, part of the image will be out of focus.

Fort Ross State Historic Park (31)

Fort Ross was a Russian settlement (the name is derived from *Rossiia,* a derivation itself of "Russia") established in 1812 by the Russian-American Company, a commercial fur hunting and trading company chartered by the tsarist government. The Russians decimated the local marine mammal population, especially sea otters, and deserted the settlement in 1841. There is one remaining original structure,

called the Rotchev House, which was built in 1836; the other buildings as well as the outer wall are replicas.

Aside from photographing the building exteriors, I enjoyed photographing the interiors, where artifacts have been placed to make the rooms look as though they are still being used today. There are old tools, furniture, muskets, coils of rope, and other objects that make very interesting vignettes. I used available light filtering in from the open doors or windows, which gave the images a soft side light.

I have visited Fort Ross a couple of times, and it has always been sunny and bright which makes photographing the exterior of the buildings difficult. Maybe you will be lucky enough to have a foggy or cloudy day, which will certainly produce better exterior images. If you arrive too early in the morning, before the park opens, it will not be possible to photograph the buildings inside the walls.

Tip: I try to avoid using my flash in interior situations since a flash casts shadows that detract from the scene. Also, the bright light of the flash will reflect off of any metal or shiny object. If you have to use a flash because it is too dark, try to

Sandstone formations at Gerstle Cove

bounce it off of the ceiling or one of the walls so that you have a softer, reflected light.

Directions: Two locations afford good overall photographs of the fort. The first is up Fort Ross Road, located directly across from the entrance. Drive up this road, through the redwoods, for 1.2 miles to a metal gate. Next to the gate is a small sign that says STATE PROPERTY. Go around or over the gate, walk about 100 yards, and bear right to a bluff that overlooks the ocean. Soon you will see Fort Ross spread out below you, with the Pacific Ocean in the background.

The second location, which I prefer and which is easier, is at the northern edge of the Russian cemetery, located just south of the fort off Highway 1. As you drive south, you will see a small turnout and the entrance to the cemetery with redwood Russian crosses. Walk north to the back of the cemetery, and you will have an excellent overview of the fort.

Jenner and the Mouth of the Russian River (32)

My favorite view of the dramatic Russian River estuary is just north of the very small town of Jenner. There is a large turnout on the west side of Highway 1, and the mouth of the river is below you. Walk along this turnout to find different angles to photograph the river with the Pacific Ocean in the background. The best time to shoot is the morning since the sun is facing the scene, lighting it up, whereas in the afternoon the sun causes harsh backlighting. Cloudy or foggy days with some visibility

Mouth of the Russian River

and sunset could also be good times to photograph this area.

From this same turnout you also have a good view north along the rugged coastline, dotted with large sea stacks.

Sonoma Coast State Beach (33)

As you drive the 13-mile stretch of Highway 1 between Jenner and Bodega Bay, there are numerous pullouts for a variety of beaches, all of which are part of Sonoma Coast State Beach. I have visited several of these and do not have a particular favorite since so many of them offer good viewpoints. If you are driving this remote coastline, I suggest that you try several of these beaches, and look for one with views to the north. In the winter and spring months a variety of wildflowers come into bloom along the bluffs overlooking the ocean, and these can provide a nice foreground for scenic shots taken with a wide-angle lens. I also look for dramatic waves splashing against the rocks and sea stacks. Note: Take care when visiting these beaches. Like most north-coast beaches, Sonoma Coast is **NOT FOR SWIMMING.** Strong rip currents, heavy surf, and sudden ground swells make the ocean extremely dangerous. Keep children back from the highest water line, and don't turn your back to the ocean. Also be careful when on bluffs and rocks. The ground is unstable and unsafe for climbing, so stay on the trails and heed warning signs.

Bodega Bay (34)

There are two locations around the area of Bodega Bay that I recommend: **Bodega Dunes** and **Bodega Head.** Bodega Dunes comprises approximately 900 acres and is located northwest of Bodega Harbor. These dunes support several grasses, in-cluding the large European beach grass which is nonnative but fun to photograph. The original native grasses were eliminated early in the 20th century by overgrazing cattle. I prefer to visit the dune area in the spring when wildflowers are blooming and on foggy or misty mornings. A hiking trail connects Bodega Dunes with the Bodgea Head, but be warned that this trail can often be very windy and cold. The high bluffs along this trail offer great views of the ocean and sea stacks below. Bodega Head is also a great location for whale watching during the winter months. In April the cow/calf pairs of gray whales are the last to migrate back to Alaska from Mexico and often swim much closer to the shoreline to avoid the orcas. I have seen them very close to shore in shallow coves, where they will stop to nurse and rest.

Bodega Harbor and the town of **Bodega Bay** also provide opportunities to photograph fishing boats and some older coastal bungalows. Look for the Bodega Bay Union Church, which was built in 1910 and has exposed rafters and a gabled roof. The Potter School, which is now a restaurant, was used in the Alfred Hitchcock film *The Birds.*

Tomales Bay (35)

Tomales Bay is 13 miles long, and Highway 1 closely follows the eastern shoreline for about 10 of those miles. Because Tomales Bay is only about 10 feet deep, it changes dramatically with the tides. At low tide vast stretches of mudflats are visible, and I have taken several interesting photographs of old piers or just sticks rising from the mud and shallow water. When the light is softened either by fog or the early or late hour, these abstracts have

Old pier on Tomales Bay

a haunting quality about them—they feel old and forgotten.

Pacific oysters are extensively raised in Tomales Bay, and there are some unique photo opportunities of the oyster racks and the interesting houses lining the bay. Tomales Bay has avoided the crushing effects of urbanization and retains a quiet, peaceful feeling that is not common in California today.

Point Reyes Lighthouse and Drake's Estero (36)

It is a beautiful drive from Point Reyes Station out Sir Francis Drake Boulevard to the Point Reyes Lighthouse and headlands, especially in the spring when the hillsides are carpeted with wildflowers. The road passes through rolling green hills and a series of dairy farms. On the way to the lighthouse you will pass Drake's Estero, the largest saltwater lagoon in Marin County. It is also very shallow, like Tomales Bay, and at low tide extensive mudflats are exposed. I found a couple of interesting photographs of the grasses and marshes at sunset. Since the water is calm, clouds reflect very well in it, and I always enjoy the effect of taking photographs of reflected clouds with the clouds that are making the reflections above them. Again, this is a situation where a two-stop neutral-density filter might be useful to bring out the foreground.

Driving farther on Sir Francis Drake Boulevard will bring you to the Point Reyes Lighthouse. This lighthouse is dramatically positioned at the tip of the Point Reyes Headlands and is very difficult to photograph. There is a long stairway—about 400 steps—going down to the platform that the lighthouse is constructed on. Once you get to the platform, you cannot stand very far back from the lighthouse, so you need a wide-angle lens such as a 20mm or 24mm to be able to frame it. There are a couple of good locations along the stairway to stop and take photographs of the lighthouse as you are walking down to it.

The granite cliffs that line the walkway down to the lighthouse are covered with striking orange algae that I first thought was lichen. I took several photographs of the algae and included some of the granite rock face in the images for contrast.

The Marin Headlands and the Golden Gate Bridge (37)

I have several favorite places where I like to photograph the Golden Gate Bridge and the city of San Francisco. One is **Conzelman Road** in the Marin Headlands. Conzelman Road is the last exit off of Highway 101 southbound or the first exit after the Golden Gate Bridge on the north side. For great viewpoints, drive a couple of miles west into Golden Gate National Recreation Area, and there are several turnouts where the Golden Gate Bridge is below you in San Francisco Bay, with the city behind it. There are multiple interesting turnouts, so don't just stop at one and think you have the only shot. These are great locations at dusk as the lights of the city come up and there is still some light in the sky. They are also good in foggy conditions, which occur quite frequently in the summer months. This is a difficult shot on a clear day in the morning after

the sun has risen because the sun will be in your face, behind the bridge. If you can get there early, just before or just after the sun rises, the light can be very dramatic, but it changes quickly, so scout out a location the night before with a compass. This is also a good location from which to photograph the rising moon behind the Golden Gate Bridge.

Tip: If the sky is brighter than the foreground, you might want to use a two- to three-stop split neutral-density filter.

Point Reyes Lighthouse

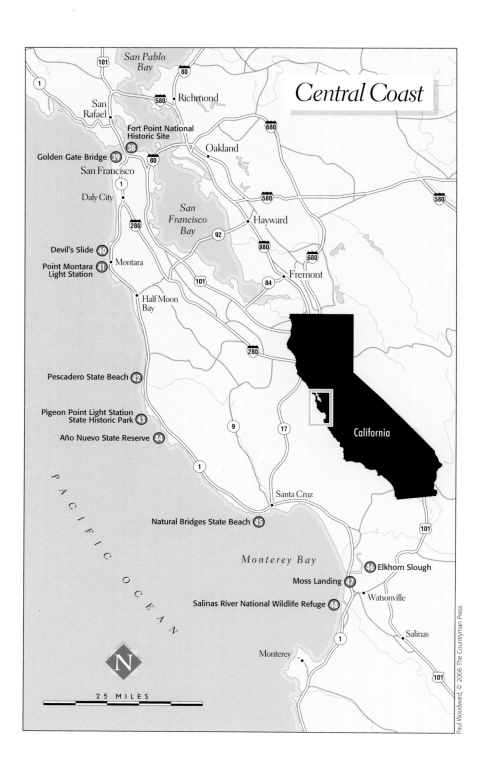

Central Coast

San Pablo Bay

101

80

1

580 Richmond

San Rafael

680

Fort Point National Historic Site

38

Oakland

Golden Gate Bridge 39

80

San Francisco

1

Daly City

580

580

San Francisco Bay

Hayward

280

92

880

Devil's Slide 40

Point Montara Light Station 41

Montara

101

84

680

Fremont

Half Moon Bay

280

Pescadero State Beach 42

Pigeon Point Light Station State Historic Park 43

9

17

California

Año Nuevo State Reserve 44

1

101

Santa Cruz

Natural Bridges State Beach 45

Monterey Bay

Elkhorn Slough 46

Moss Landing 47

Watsonville

Salinas River National Wildlife Refuge 48

Salinas

1

Monterey

101

P A C I F I C   O C E A N

N

25 MILES

Paul Woodward, © 2006 The Countryman Press

Central Coast—San Francisco to Morro Bay

Golden Gate Bridge from Fort Point (38)

As you drive south on Highway 101, Fort Point is the first exit on the San Francisco side of the Golden Gate Bridge and offers stunning close-up views of the bridge. There is a visitors center and vista point above the fort, which offers a good view of the towers and cables of the bridge. As you leave the visitors center, turn left on Lincoln Boulevard, and turn left again on Long Avenue, which will take you down to Marine Drive, which goes along the waterfront below the Golden Gate Bridge. You can walk along Marine Drive to get different perspectives, but they are all looking up at the bridge toward Marin County. This is a good location when there is fog and the bridge is partly obscured. A museum, bookstore, and small coffee shop offer solace on cold, foggy mornings.

Golden Gate Bridge from Langdon Court and the Coastal Trail (39)

From Fort Point get back on Lincoln Boulevard, and drive south toward Golden Gate Park. Shortly after crossing Highway 101, there is a right turn called Langdon Court, which becomes a paved parking lot with a good view of the Golden Gate Bridge. I particularly like this location because there are trees that can be included in the photograph that give an additional point of interest by providing a foreground. You can frame the bridge with trees, or have them coming in from one side or the other. Walk around, take your time, and different compositions will become apparent to you.

A little farther down Lincoln is another turnout named Bowley Street that will lead you to a coastline trail. From this trail you can walk down to the water and include the shoreline and waves in photographs, with the Golden Gate Bridge in the background. I have seen quite a few images taken from the beach, and they are quite strong. It is helpful to have a detailed map of the city of San Francisco, with all these turnouts and roads clearly marked.

Devil's Slide (40)

As you drive south on Highway 1 through San Francisco, you will leave the city in 30 to 45 minutes. Then continue driving through the small town of Pacifica until you arrive at Devil's Slide, a spectacular example of uplifted rock layers that are very old seafloor sediment. These layers—pushed up at 45 degrees and called the Franciscan Formations—were created when the Pacific Plate and the North American Plate slipped over each other and pushed these sedimentary layers up at radical angles. The area where these two plates meet and continue to move today is the San Andreas Fault, a major earthquake zone that runs the length of California. The Devil's Slide area is very active, and this section of Highway 1 is often closed during periods of heavy rainfall when landslides frequently occur. Devil's

Golden Gate Bridge from the Coastal Trail

Slide is not a particularly strong photograph, but I always enjoy visiting areas that make me wish I had taken more geology classes in college.

Montara Lighthouse (41)

The Montara Lighthouse, which is on the National Register of Historic Places, is not as dramatic as the Pigeon Point Lighthouse (43) farther to the south, but it is worth a visit. The Montara Lighthouse is a New England–style lighthouse: much shorter in height, and sometimes the lighthouse is incorporated into the lighthouse keeper's residence. A detached Victorian-style house next to the lighthouse is now a hostel with nice facilities, including a hot tub. As with all West Coast lighthouses, the best time for photographs is late afternoon as the sun is low on the horizon. This gives a soft side light, which is much more pleasing than when the sun is high in the sky.

Pescadero State Beach and Natural Preserve (42)

Between Pigeon Point Lighthouse to the south and Half Moon Bay to the north lie a series of beautiful beaches, some with parking lots and others with just turnouts known to the locals. I like the mile-long Pescadero Beach where Pescadero Creek flows into the ocean at the north end and combines with Butano Creek to form a large marsh and slough. Aside from the several good locations for photography on the bluffs above the creek and ocean, the marsh below is an excellent place to explore and look for wildlife with a telephoto lens. In the spring blue herons nest here in the eucalyptus trees, and during mating season, their plumage is much more developed and striking. Many other species of birds include egrets and the occasional peregrine falcon. I always find something interesting to photograph in this area, whether it is the streams flowing into the ocean or some of the birds located upstream.

The 2-mile drive to the nearby town of Pescadero is just far enough off Highway 1 to keep it remote and authentic as a Portuguese-Italian farming community. Just outside of Pescadero to the east is the largest Monterey cypress tree in the United States, with a trunk over 40 feet in circumference. And if you are visiting the small town of Pescadero, be sure to stop at Duarte's Restaurant, well-known to both locals and visitors.

Pigeon Point Lighthouse (43)

One of the most picturesque and photographed lighthouses along the California coastline, Pigeon Point is located along Highway 1 approximately midway between Santa Cruz and Half Moon Bay. There are several excellent locations for photographing this lighthouse, and my current favorite is the first unmarked turnout to the south of the lighthouse, just off Highway 1. A small dirt area has enough space for several cars to park. Often fishermen park here and walk out to the rocks overlooking the ocean. After you park, walk back toward the lighthouse, and you will come to a bluff that puts the ocean and some rocks in the foreground and you are close enough that the lighthouse does not disappear in the image. (If you drive to one of the turnouts farther south along Highway 1, I think you will be too far from the lighthouse, and it becomes a small part of the image.) I have also seen nice photographs taken of the lighthouse from the parking lot to the north. In these there is less foreground, but the lighthouse is much larger in the picture.

Tip: In January and February the ground is covered with bright-yellow flowers; at other times you will hopefully find a cloudy evening with a dramatic sunset. Even if the conditions are not perfect, Pigeon Point Lighthouse always provides a strong and compelling image.

Año Nuevo State Reserve (44)

Año Nuevo is located 27 miles south of Half Moon Bay on Highway 1 and is well-known as a protected breeding ground for the northern elephant seal. The only way to visit the beach areas where the elephant seals come ashore is on a guided tour, and more information about these tours is available at 800-444-4445. These walking tours are about 3 miles long, take about two and a half hours, and are not cancelled due to bad weather. It can be cold and wet, so be prepared with warm clothes and a rain jacket or umbrella.

Female elephant seal at
Año Nuevo State Reserve

The large male elephant seals reach a length of 14 to 16 feet and can weigh up to 3 tons. The smaller females reach 10 to 12 feet in length and weigh 1,200 to 2,000 pounds. Their name comes from the inflatable nasal sac (proboscis) that hangs down the front of the mature bull's face, resembling an elephant's trunk. The males begin arriving in late November and often have brief and bloody battles to establish a hierarchy and take control of a harem of females. Like most mammals, they don't mate for life. The stronger and more aggressive males get to do most of the breeding and are continually being challenged by growing adolescent males. The females arrive in early December and begin giving birth to pups that weigh 75 pounds and grow to 300 to 400 pounds within a month. The actual mating takes place about 24 days after the birth of the pups, and gestation is about eight months. A natural delay allows the fertilized egg to implant in the uterus so that the birthing will take place at the same time the following year.

Cameras and tripods are permitted on the guided tours, and I highly recommend this trip if you can be in the area at the right time. Bring a telephoto lens, and be prepared to take a lot of pictures. Hopefully you will get to see the drama of two large bulls charging each other, and if this is what you are after, it is best to arrive early in the season. Check the weather forecast before you go so that you know what to expect; but then again, how often are the forecasts correct? It is best to be prepared for cold, wet weather. As you drive south along Highway 1, there are many small beaches known to the local surfers. You will see their cars parked alongside the road, and if you enjoy taking pictures of surfers with a telephoto lens, just park and follow the paths to the ocean. A couple of nude beaches can be found along this stretch of Highway 1 as well as south of Big Sur; these are *not* good locations for telephoto lenses.

Natural Bridges State Beach (45)

Natural Bridges State Beach is located a couple of miles south of Santa Cruz on West Cliff Drive. There is a parking lot above the natural bridge, but I think the best view of the arch is from the beach below. This is an interesting photograph, and I would look for a day when there are clouds in the sky to add interest. Above the beach is a boardwalk through the **Butterfly Natural Preserve.** Monarch butterflies spend October through February on the eucalyptus trees located in the park. If the temperature is below 55 degrees, the butterflies are very lethargic and not very colorful, but on most afternoons they can be seen in large groups in the trees with their wings spread open and fluttering. A telephoto lens is needed to get a good shot since they are up high; I recommend at least a 400mm lens. For more information on the Butterfly Natural Preserve, call 408-423-4609 or 408-429-2850.

Directions: As you drive south on Highway 1, turn south toward the ocean on Swift Drive. Swift Drive dead-ends at West Cliff Drive. Turn right on West Cliff, and follow the signs to Natural Bridges.

Elkhorn Slough National Estuarine Research and State Ecological Reserve (46)

Elkhorn Slough includes 1,400 acres of scarce wetlands and dry lands and continues for several miles inland from the

Monarchs at Natural Bridges State Beach

coast. Over 90 percent of the wetlands on the West Coast have been lost to development, which makes the Elkhorn Slough habitat unique and extremely important to migrating birds and other wildlife. The best way to explore the slough is on a pontoon boat tour with Elkhorn Slough Safari Nature Tours. The boat gives you a stable, dry, and elevated platform to photograph from. They are very accommodating to photographers and even have special photographers' tours. For more information about these tours call 831-633-5555.

When I went on one of these tours I used my 400mm telephoto and was able to get some very good shots of the sea otters.

Another way to visit is to rent a kayak at one of the locations on the west side of Highway 1 and paddle into the slough. This allows you to get close to a large variety of birds, sea otters, and seals—more seals are present in the summer months when they are pupping and molting. (A great kayaking option is to drive to Kirby Park on the northeast side of the slough, rent a kayak there, and paddle one way back to the harbor.) But if you kayak, watch the weather and tide changes. When it is windy in the slough, it can be difficult to paddle; it is also difficult to paddle against the tide. I have been caught trying to paddle out when the tide is coming in full force, and it takes much more effort. Also, if you paddle inland during a high tide and the tide recedes, you could become stranded in the mud, so use caution and stay alert to the changing conditions. Having said all this, kayaking in the slough is a great experience with lots to see. Look for the many blue and great herons along with pelicans just waiting to be photographed. For more information about Elkhorn Slough, visit the Web site of the Elkhorn Slough Foundation at www.elkhornslough.org.

If you don't want to kayak or go on a pontoon boat, it is easy to visit the slough on the many hiking trails.

Tip: If you explore the slough in a kayak, be careful with your camera equipment. I always take several large Ziploc-type baggies, one or two towels, and a waterproof bag to carry the equipment.

Directions: The visitors center is located on Elkhorn Road, which is reached by turning east on Dolan Road off Highway 1. (Kirby Park is located beyond the visitors center off of Elkhorn Road.) Go past the power plant, and take a left on Elkhorn Road. Call 408-728-2822 for information.

Across Highway 1 from Elkhorn Slough is **Moss Landing State Beach.** This is a good place to park to explore the area, but I find the slough area more interesting for photography than the beach.

Moss Landing (47)

Moss Landing is a small, picturesque coastal village with many antiques shops, good restaurants, and a very scenic waterfront. Unfortunately it is located across Highway 1 from a large power plant that dominates the skyline. Still, I always find Moss Landing an interesting place to explore for photographs of boats, fishing nets, and old buildings in various states of disrepair. This is a colorful and authentic waterfront that does not attract as many tourists as other areas along the coast. In the spring fields of flowers are usually growing up to the edge of the water and provide a nice foreground with boats in the background.

Salinas River Wildlife Refuge (48)

A wide trail through the refuge takes you to the Salinas River estuary, a good location for spotting and photographing birds. As you approach the beach, the sand dunes on both sides of the trail have barriers to keep you from walking on them. From April to June this is an active breeding area for the western snowy plover, and there are many of them to be seen in the dunes. They run from their nests to lead you and other predators away from them. I have visited this dune area many times and have also found several good locations for photographs of wind patterns in the sand. These wind patterns are best photographed late in the day, when the afternoon sun casts shadows from the ripples.

As you continue along the trail and arrive at the beach, you can walk either direction. If you go to the right, you will soon come to an old shipwreck at the mouth of the Salinas River. The walk down the secluded beach is worth the photograph, especially on a foggy day or in the evening. If you go to the left, toward Monterey, you will have a long, solitary walk along a surprisingly secluded beach area with many interesting photo opportunities. This is a great location to photograph either the sunrise or the rising moon.

Tip: The best time to photograph the rising moon is the evening before the actual full moon. The night before a full moon, the moon rises while there is still light in the sky so that you can include the landscape in the foreground with the moon in the background. I prefer to use about a 300mm lens to make the moon appear large but not too large.

Directions: From Highway 1, north or south, take the Del Monte exit and turn west, toward the ocean. Driving south, the turn is just after the Salinas River. As you follow Del Monte west, it soon turns into a dirt road and goes between two artichoke fields. Follow the dirt road for about a quarter mile and park in the lot. Then walk through the gate, turn left, and follow the road for about a half mile. The large dunes to the left are Martin Dunes—valuable habitat for a wide variety of flora and fauna.

Dunes at Salinas River Wildlife Refuge

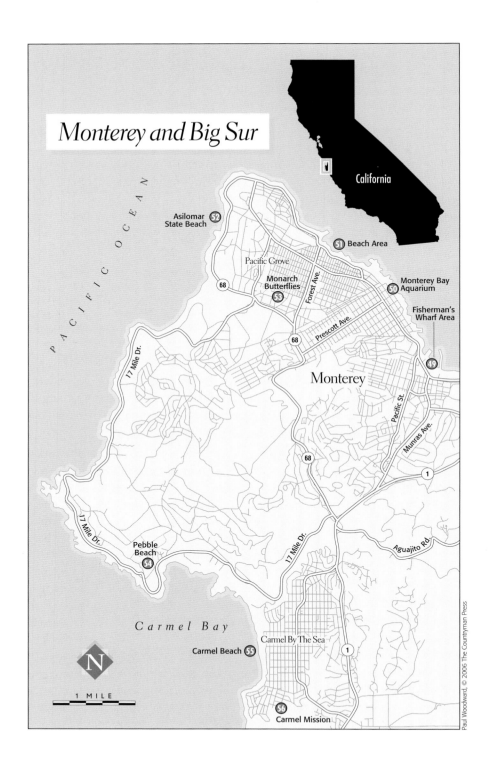

Monterey and Big Sur

California

Asilomar State Beach 52

51 Beach Area

Pacific Grove

68

Monarch Butterflies 53

Forest Ave.

50 Monterey Bay Aquarium

Fisherman's Wharf Area

68

Prescott Ave.

49

Monterey

PACIFIC OCEAN

17 Mile Dr.

Pacific St.

Munras Ave.

68

1

17 Mile Dr.

17 Mile Dr.

Aguajito Rd.

Pebble Beach 54

Carmel Bay

Carmel Beach 55

Carmel By The Sea

1

N

1 MILE

56

Carmel Mission

Paul Woodward, © 2006 The Countryman Press

Monterey and Big Sur Area

Fisherman's Wharf (49)

Fisherman's Wharf in Monterey is one of the most photogenic wharfs in all of California. Originally built in 1846, it was used extensively in the early 20th century when fishing in Monterey Bay was a large industry. Today there are two wharfs; one is dedicated to restaurants and tourist attractions, while the second is still an active dock for many commercial fishing boats. Both wharfs are colorful locations, with many types of scenes to be photographed.

My favorite spot to photograph the wharf is from along the **Recreational Trail,** which parallels the coastline for several miles. Generally I walk along the trail to a location where I can photograph the moored boats in the foreground and the colorful buildings on the wharf in the background. At low tide many rocks are exposed, and these rocks are always used by local harbor seals to dry and sun themselves, adding another element to be photographed. A short walk south along the Recreational Trail will take you to the Coast Guard Pier, which has a large stone breakwater that is always covered with sea lions.

The Rec Trail is also a great location to photograph either sunrise or rising moon shots since you are facing east. Sunrise shots are most effective about 20 minutes before the sun rises over the horizon and on days when there are lots of clouds. For rising moon shots I go out the night before the full moon since it appears while there is still light in the sky. I try to stand back so that I can use a small telephoto lens, such as a 300mm. This makes the moon appear large but not so large that it is unrealistic. The Rec Trail is also my favorite spot for photographing Fourth of July fireworks. Unfortunately, it is often foggy along the Monterey coastline in the summer, including the Fourth of July, so watch the weather forecast. Early evening is a great time to catch the lights from the restaurants reflected in the water.

Walking onto either wharf, I often find good shots of pelicans, seagulls, lots of sea lions, and the occasional sea otter. There are also many large and comfortable boats that offer whale watching, which is particularly good in December and January, when the gray whales are migrating south down to Baja, or in March and April, when they are returning to Alaska.

Tip: When photographing fireworks, set your camera on a tripod and use a fairly wide-angle lens, such as a 35mm. Aim your camera where you think the fireworks will occur, and focus on infinity. I then set my camera to "bulb," which allows you to hold open the shutter for as long as you want. I open the shutter as the fireworks are launched and hold it open until they stop. This may take 15 to 30 seconds, but you get the bright trails of the fireworks instead of just a quick snapshot. I use a cable release or a newer electronic shutter release that allows me to control the shutter opening.

Monterey Bay Aquarium (50)

Taking photographs in the aquarium is not particularly difficult or technical, but there are a few guidelines that will help your images. You are allowed to use a tripod and flash, but these are not very helpful in many situations. I have had better luck either using ISO 800 film or just pushing the ISO on my digital camera to 800. If you do use a flash, be sure you stand off to the side of the image so that the flash is not reflected in the acrylic windows. When I use a tripod, I keep the ball head adjusted so that I can move the camera fairly easily to follow the fish. You'll enjoy photographing in the main aquarium area, but watch for the strong light coming down into the water. My favorite location is the jellyfish tanks. You have to wait a while for a good composition to appear, but the orange jellyfish in the blue water always makes a strong image.

Photographing in the aquarium has made me realize the benefits of using a digital camera. First of all I can see how the images are turning out, and in this difficult environment this is a significant benefit. Secondly it is easy to adjust the ISO to a higher number in situations where it is needed, rather than changing rolls of film. This is much easier than ex-

perimenting with different films with different ISOs, which I have done in past years. Also, I think digital cameras perform better than film cameras in low-light situations such as the aquarium. If you are new to digital photography, this is a good place to use it and experiment with different settings.

Tip: The Monterey Bay Aquarium is a very popular tourist destination on the Monterey Peninsula, so I recommend arriving early on a weekday to avoid the large crowds. This will make your picture-taking experience much better.

Directions: The Monterey Bay Aquarium is a landmark on the Monterey Peninsula, and there are many signs leading you to it. It is located at the end of Cannery Row, directly on Monterey Bay. If you are arriving on Highway 1, I suggest taking the Munras exit and driving west for about a mile to Fisherman's Wharf. Once you arrive at Fisherman's Wharf, turn south on Del Monte, the main street that parallels the shoreline, and follow it through the tunnel. As you exit the tunnel, stay to the right, and try to end up on Wave Street. It is a few blocks to the aquarium, and there are several parking lots within easy walking distance. I usually avoid parking on the street since there is a time limit, and you want to be relaxed while walking through the aquarium.

Beach Area in Pacific Grove (51)

The 3-mile beach area along Pacific Grove offers a wide range of photographic possibilities. The first area is Lover's Point, a large rock outcropping where there are often surfers and kayakers. Continue along Ocean View as it follows the ocean, and there will be numerous

Jellyfish at the Monterey Bay Aquarium

Sea figs carpet the beach in Pacific Grove

turnouts with spectacular ocean views and eroded rocks in the foreground. This area is particularly dramatic during winter storms, at sunset, and from April through July when the ground is carpeted with sea figs, a bright-pink flowering groundcover. At low tide there are many tide pools to explore, with starfish, anemones, and many other tidal inhabitants. I like the first two or three turnouts because of the large rock formations, which turn a nice brown color in late afternoon.

As you drive south along Ocean View Boulevard, you will see Point Pinos Lighthouse on the left. It can be reached by making a left turn on Lighthouse Avenue. The lighthouse has restricted hours, but it is possible to get some very good shots of it even when the grounds are closed. Shortly beyond Lighthouse Avenue is Asilomar State Beach.

Directions: From the Monterey Bay Aquarium, continue on Wave Street, which becomes Ocean View Boulevard, the main street that goes along the ocean in Pacific Grove. From Highway 1 turn west on Highway 68, and follow it about 4.5 miles through Pacific Grove to Ocean View Boulevard. Highway 68 becomes Forest Avenue as it goes through the small town of Pacific Grove and dead-ends at the beach. Take a left on Ocean View, and follow it along the Pacific Ocean.

Asilomar State Beach (52)

Asilomar State Beach extends for about a mile along the Pacific Grove coastline, and a portion of it is across the street from

Ice plants contrast with rocks on this stretch of Asilomar State Beach

Asilomar Conference Grounds. I particularly like to photograph this area at sunset, when the small creeks are running into the ocean and the water reflects the red and orange colors of the sky. The creeks provide leading lines and reflections, especially when there are brightly colored clouds.

Monarch Butterflies in Pacific Grove (53)

Pacific Grove is also known as "Butterfly Town" due to the large number of monarch butterflies that migrate and spend the winter months. The butterflies begin arriving in October and are well settled in by Thanksgiving. The best time to view them is in the afternoon when the temperature warms up, and they begin moving around.

The many thousands of monarchs stay in the area until February or March, until their mating season is over, and then they leave, returning north all the way to the Canadian Rockies and southern Alaska.

Tip: Don't forget to try your flash with the monarch butterflies. I usually adjust my flash down about one to one and a half stops so that it is not so bright but still lights up the image.

Directions: From Highway 1 take Highway 68 west, and continue down the hill for about 4 miles to Lighthouse Avenue. Take a left at the stop sign on Lighthouse, and continue for about 1 mile to Ridge Road. Turn left onto Ridge, and follow the signs to the Monarch Grove Sanctuary, which is a right-hand turn off Ridge.

Pebble Beach, Seventeen Mile Drive (54)

Seventeen Mile Drive is the main route through Pebble Beach and takes you to all of the interesting areas to photograph. There are many gated entrances into Pebble Beach, and an entry fee is charged. The main entrance is a turn off Highway 1 between Monterey and Carmel. Follow Seventeen Mile Drive past the Pebble Beach Lodge, and about 1 mile farther to Pescadero Point. There are many places to park along both sides of the road and many striking cypress trees along the coastline with arresting angles. This location is best at sunset on a partly cloudy day since the setting sun behind the trees provides a colorful background. I also like these trees on foggy summer days, a condition that allow for mysterious-looking images.

A little farther along Seventeen Mile Drive is the **Lone Cypress Tree,** the iconographic image of Pebble Beach. This tree is best photographed in the evening, just before or after sunset when there is color in the sky. Also, the rock beneath the tree, normally a gray color, turns rich brown as the horizontal light sweeps across it. Images of this tree are copyrighted by the Pebble Beach Company, and you should check with them before you publish or sell them.

Continuing along Seventeen Mile Drive past Cypress Point, there is a long beach area that eventually leads to Spanish Bay and the Pacific Grove Gate, or exit. There are many locations to take photographs along this beautiful coastline. Each time I go, I find something new and striking. Again, I prefer to visit this

The Pacific backdrops the seventh green at famed Pebble Beach.

area in late afternoon because the setting sun provides a strong sidelight on the rocks and beaches.

Directions: I prefer to enter Pebble Beach through the Carmel Gate, which is at the bottom of Ocean Avenue. From Highway 1, turn west at the Ocean Avenue stoplight, and drive through Carmel for approximately 1 mile. Take the last right turn onto San Antonio, which will curve around to the left to the Pebble Beach entrance gate. (There is a fee to enter Pebble Beach.) From the gate, follow the curves up the hill, and take a left on Seventeen Mile Drive.

Carmel Beach (55)

Carmel Beach is worthy of its reputation as one of the most beautiful beaches on the coast. The curved shoreline has striking views to the north of the Pebble Beach Lodge and the famous Pebble Beach golf course. There are often surfers at Carmel Beach, and it is a favorite of all of the local dogs (and their owners) since they are allowed to run freely.

Carmel Beach at low tide

One of my favorite spots to photograph Carmel Beach is reached by driving south on Scenic Drive for about a half mile until you can look back and see the entire beach, with Pebble Beach golf course and lodge in the background. However, numerous places along the walking trail and on the beach itself offer interesting photographs. There are many old cypress trees, which can frame your shot. In the evening I have often photographed surfers silhouetted against the colorful red sky.

Directions: From Highway 1 turn west at the stoplight for Ocean Avenue, and drive downhill for approximately 1 mile. There is a parking lot at the bottom of Ocean Avenue. To drive along the beach, you have to go back up the hill to the first right on San Antonio. After two blocks turn right again on Eighth, then left on Scenic. Scenic follows Carmel Beach for approximately 1 mile, with parking along the side of the road. It's fun to try to guess the value of the beautiful homes that are located along Scenic Drive.

Carmel Mission (56)

For photographers this is an exceptional mission, with its lush gardens, bell tower, and two fountains. I can offer a few suggestions for locations, but you will find many interesting photographs by taking your time and walking around.

As you enter the mission, there is a fountain to the right, and I like to include this fountain and the flowers around it in the foreground with the bell tower and façade in the background. It can be frustrating to wait for all of the tourists to walk out of your frame, which is a good reason to avoid the mission in the middle of the day. From here, walk into the back court-

The Carmel Mission

yard to a second fountain, which again can be included in the foreground with the bell tower in the background. Also, on this side of the mission is a wall with a stairway that often has beautiful flowers growing on it; I have taken many detail-type shots that incorporate this stairway. Then look down the outside corridors with the repeating columns. Many missions have this type of architecture, and I particularly like the receding lines at this one.

I have also taken some nice shots of the stucco roof and bell tower from outside the mission walls. You will see these shots from the road that runs perpendicular to Rio Road along the side of the mission. I particularly like this location at sunset, when the stucco takes on a golden glow. If you follow this road that runs beside the mission, you will soon come to Clint Eastwood's well-known Mission Ranch. The Mission Ranch restaurant has out-

door seating that overlooks a beautiful meadow than ends at the beach of Carmel Bay and is a great place to relax with a glass of wine at sunset. If you don't want to miss the opportunity to photograph at sunset, you can take pictures of the grasses in the meadow in front of you while you enjoy your wine.

Across the street from the Carmel Mission is one of Carmel's well-known thatched-roof cottages. There are usually flowers growing in the front yard, making this cottage a particularly nice photograph on a cloudy day or early morning or early evening.

Directions: The Carmel Mission is located just a few blocks west of Highway 1 on Rio Road. While you are in the area, you can go the other direction on Rio Road to one of my favorite restaurants, the Rio Grill.

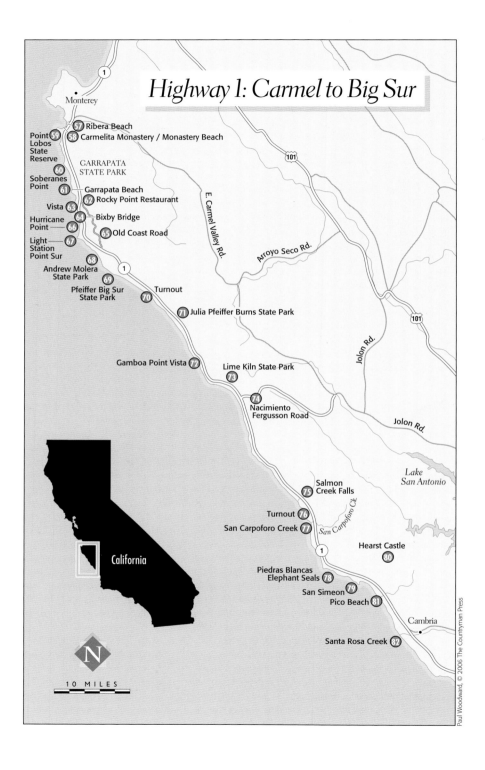

Highway 1: Carmel to Big Sur

Monterey

57 Ribera Beach
Point Lobos State Reserve 59 58 Carmelita Monastery / Monastery Beach

GARRAPATA STATE PARK

Soberanes Point 60
61 Garrapata Beach
Vista 63 62 Rocky Point Restaurant
Hurricane Point 64 Bixby Bridge
66 65 Old Coast Road
Light Station Point Sur 67

Andrew Molera State Park 68

69 Pfeiffer Big Sur State Park
70 Turnout

71 Julia Pfeiffer Burns State Park

Gamboa Point Vista 72
73 Lime Kiln State Park

74 Nacimiento Fergusson Road

E. Carmel Valley Rd.
Arroyo Seco Rd.
Jolon Rd.
Jolon Rd.

Lake San Antonio

75 Salmon Creek Falls

Turnout 76
San Carpoforo Creek 77
San Carpoforo Ck.

Hearst Castle 80

Piedras Blancas Elephant Seals 78
San Simeon 79
Pico Beach 81

California

Cambria

Santa Rosa Creek 82

N

10 MILES

Paul Woodward, © 2006 The Countryman Press

Highway 1—Carmel to Big Sur

The coastline along Highway 1—the Pacific Coast Highway—between Carmel and Big Sur deserves its reputation as one of the most beautiful in the world. There are numerous turnouts where you can stop to take photographs; just look for the tripod holes. I will list some of my favorites. As you drive south through the stoplight at Rio Road on Highway 1, set your trip odometer to 0 with the mileage for these great locations from this point:

0.8 Mile: Ribera Beach (57)

Ribera Beach is not very well known, even in the Monterey area, but it is one of my favorite beach areas for photography because it has Point Lobos to the south and the Carmel River to the north.

As you approach Ribera Beach, you will see a large wooden cross on your right, marking the spot where the Portola Crespi Expedition erected a similar cross in 1769 to alert the supply ship *San Jose*. Unfortunately the *San Jose* had been lost at sea, and the supplies never arrived.

Walk on down to the beach, and there are interesting rock formations that become great tide pools at low tide. In the background is Point Lobos, and I have spent many hours at sunset lining up the rocks in the foreground with Point Lobos in the background. I also like to include texture or patterns in the sand that are created as the waves recede. At low tide there are many starfish and anemones to include in your photographs. Be very careful on the rocks as they are extremely slippery when the water recedes.

As you walk to Ribera Beach, you can also take a trail to the right, or north, which will take you to the Carmel River. This river flows only in the winter but forms an estuary all year long. Walk around and look for such birds as herons and egrets. I also like to use the flowing river as a leading line into the ocean.

Directions: After you pass Rio Road, the last stoplight on Highway 1, you will soon cross the bridge over the Carmel River.

Sunset at Ribera Beach

After 0.8 mile take a right turn onto Ribera Road. Drive about 0.5 mile to the second right-hand turn, Calle La Cruz. Park at the end of this little cul-de-sac, and the beach entrance will be to the north. Walk down the paved and gravel pathway to the beach.

1.3 Miles: Carmelite Monastery and Monastery Beach (58)

The monastery, which is set back in the hills above the ocean, and its beach, on the west side of the road, make nice photographs later in the day. Standing on Monastery Beach, which is a favorite with scuba divers, Point Lobos is in the background to the south. This is also a good location during winter storms as waves crash against the rocks sending spray high into the air. As you look at Point Lobos, you will notice a large rock outcropping, and one of these large granite boulders has about five Indian bedrock grinding mortars. Unfortunately, to see them close up, you have to enter Point Lobos from the main entrance, which is another mile south, and hike back to this location. San Jose Creek also runs into the ocean at this point and often attracts many birds.

2.2 Miles: Point Lobos State Reserve (59)

Point Lobos State Reserve is considered by many to be the crown jewel of the California State Parks system. It contains 554 land acres and 750 submerged acres, and it was the first underwater reserve in the nation. Point Lobos is open from 9 to 5 year-round, and the reserve is limited to 450 visitors at one time, so occasionally on busy weekends, there is a line to enter. (For more information, call 831-624-4909.)

There are numerous hiking trails within the park, some following the coastline and some going through the Monterey pine forests. I encourage all visitors to explore the park and discover their personal favorite spots for photography; however, I can recommend the following locations in particular.

As you enter Point Lobos there is a turn to the right to **Whaler's Cove.** This is a great location for photographing sea otters, seals, and birds, including blue herons, great egrets, and snowy egrets. If you follow the trail to the west from Whaler's Cove, you will come to one of several large colonies of cormorants; with luck, you will get to see their elaborate mating dances. Whaler's Cove is the scuba diving location for Point Lobos, and the parking lot is often full of divers and kayakers. Just up the trail is the Whaler's Cabin, which houses the Whaling Station Museum—well worth the visit to get a sense of the whaling that took place along the Pacific coastline in the 19th century. In the spring it is easy to

Great blue heron at Whaler's Cove, Point Lobos State Reserve

China Cove at Point Lobos State Reserve

spot harbor seals with their pups on the shoreline below. Although you cannot approach the seals, you can get very good shots with a telephoto lens. I have also photographed nesting blue herons in this location, as seen on page 60.

After Whaler's Cove, get back in your car and drive to the first parking lot near the Information Station. The park docents here can answer many of your questions and make helpful suggestions about which trails to hike. I like the Cypress Grove Trail for great shots of the cypress trees and the coastline. You can also take the next trail to the right, which brings you to an overlook for the Old Veterans Tree, a large cypress with dramatic exposed roots. I usually find deer in this area, and they are very used to people and

to being photographed, so this may be an opportunity for a great close-up image.

After exploring this area, drive south along the ocean to visit **Weston Beach.** There is always something to photograph at this great location, be it a close-up of the eroded rocks or multicolored rock layers. At low tide look for starfish and other tide pool sea life. Weston Beach is also a great location for sunset photographs, but since the park closes at 5 p.m. year-round, these shots are only available in the winter. I try to get there as close to December 21, the shortest day, as possible.

The next stop is the southernmost parking area and a visit to **China Cove.** When the sun is overhead and the light is right, this cove has striking turquoise-blue water and a white sand beach. If the

Garrapata Beach

The Soberanes Canyon Trail follows Soberanes Creek for a couple of miles before turning north and becoming much steeper as it climbs to meet the Rocky Ridge Trail at the top of the hill, about 1,900 feet above sea level. The Soberanes Canyon Trail goes through a striking redwood forest and is particularly photogenic during the winter rainy season when the moss on the trees is a vivid green. The higher part of the trail is covered with flowers in March and April and is a great location for photographing California poppies and lupines.

My favorite location to photograph Soberanes Point is just across from the main parking area on the western side of the highway. A network of trails leads to bluffs overlooking the Pacific, and there are many good areas for spotting whales migrating both south and north during the winter and spring months. I always seem to find a new place to stand to take photographs of this dramatic meeting of sea and land. Late-afternoon light is best, which turns the rocks a warm brown color, and there are often large waves crashing against the isolated rocks off the coast. After the sun sets the colors change dramatically, and I have taken some nice photographs just before dark, when both the ocean and sky are a deep blue. As you explore this area, you will find the location where Soberanes Creek spills over a small cliff and creates a nice waterfall in the winter months.

water temperature weren't 55 degrees, you would think it was the Caribbean. Then hike a little farther to **Pelican Point,** where I have seen gray whales with their calves in the very shallow water, evidently avoiding the orcas, or killer whales, that hunt the calves in deeper water.

6.8 Miles: Garrapata State Park— Soberanes Point (60)

Soberanes Point is the northernmost part of Garrapata State Park and extends to both sides of Highway 1. The entrance on the east side of the highway is the beginning of two great hiking trails that actually form a loop and take you to a very high overlook point above the Pacific Ocean.

9.6 Miles: Garrapata Beach (61)

Garrapata Beach is a favorite among local photographers in the Monterey area. The triangular shaped rocks that appear in the surf at low tide have been photographed numerous times. But that should not discourage you from visiting this dramatic beach; there is always something new to be discovered and photographed.

As you drive along Highway 1, you will find the large turnout on the west side of the road, where the path that leads down to Garrapata Beach begins. This beach is one of the most photographed along the Big Sur coastline. Along with the rocks in the surf, I also like to photograph the coastline view to the south from the top of the bluff above the beach. And as you walk north along the beach, you come to a small creek, which was often photographed in the past because of the large number of calla lilies that grew along its banks. Unfortunately state park crews built a trail with a bridge that now bisects this creek and eliminates this wonderful image. And now that this trail is much more accessible, there are fewer calla lilies. Still, there are many striking areas along the beach to explore and photograph, and I always find something new and interesting. If you walk upstream along this creek and then look back at the ocean, you should be able to find a pleasing image.

10.8 Miles: Rocky Point Restaurant (62)

The driveway down to the Rocky Point Restaurant and the lower parking lot offer spectacular views looking south across fields that in the winter months are vivid green and dotted with cows. In the background are Rocky Creek Bridge and the Big Sur coastline. From the lower parking lot many short trails lead around Rocky Point. The cliffs and the blue Pacific below offer many opportunities for dramatic images, and this has always been one of my favorite locations along the Big Sur

coastline. Plus the sunsets from this location can be very colorful, with many rock outcroppings available to place in the foreground. The Rocky Point Restaurant has an outside deck with views facing the ocean—a great spot to relax before or after your photo session and enjoy the afternoon sun and a glass of wine along with lunch or dinner.

11.1 Miles: Vista from Turnout (63)

This large turnout just after the Rocky Point Restaurant has a great view to the south, which includes an arch in the rocks along the coastline and Rocky Creek Bridge in the distance. In the winter the fields in the foreground are bright green. I look for clear days with white puffy clouds, which often occur just after a storm.

13.3 Miles: Bixby Bridge (64)

It is easy to understand why Bixby Bridge is one of the most photographed locations in the world. The bridge, with its sweeping, graceful arches high above the Pacific Ocean, has been the site of numerous movies and commercials. In late-afternoon light the bridge turns warm and provides

View from Rocky Point

Bixby Bridge from Hurricane Point

an excellent photograph from the ocean side looking to the south. As you walk around, you will find other interesting perspectives and views to photograph. Bixby Bridge is the midpoint of the Big Sur Marathon that takes place along Highway 1 in April.

13.3 Miles: Old Coast Road (65)

The Old Coast Road is a 12-mile-long unpaved and often muddy road that begins at Bixby Bridge and heads east into the hills. This is the road that was used before Bixby Bridge was built, and it comes out at Andrew Molera State Park about 8 miles south on Highway 1. A sign says the road is impassable in the winter, but unless there is excessive rainfall, it is not that difficult. And wet winter days provide the best conditions to take this road to photograph the old redwood groves that are located several miles inland.

Aside from the redwoods, there is an excellent shot of Bixby Bridge about a half mile up the Old Coast Road. As the road turns south, look toward the ocean, and you will see the bridge silhouetted against the skyline. This makes a dramatic photograph at sunset or on a stormy day when there are clouds in the sky.

14.5 Miles: Hurricane Point (66)

As you continue south along Highway 1, the road climbs to Hurricane Point. There is a large turnout at the top and an often photographed scene looking north along the Big Sur coastline with Bixby Bridge. This scene looks best in the winter when the grass is green and in late afternoon when the sun is lower in the sky. I also prefer cloudy days since so much of the sky is included in the photograph. I have gone to this location quite a few times at sunset looking for the perfect light, but I have never been totally successful. Perhaps you will be lucky and get there just as the sun sets, the clouds light up, and a ray of light shines on Bixby Bridge. The large fields in front of you are part of the old Brazil Ranch, which became the Funt Ranch when Alan Funt purchased the property; they were purchased and preserved by The Big Sur Land Trust and The Nature Conservancy.

Continuing south on Highway 1, you will cross the **Little Sur River.** At 17.2 miles a turnout on the right-hand side provides an excellent view of the river, the beach, and a hillside in the background. I try to stop at this location every time I drive south on Highway 1 because it is always different. A large area of ice plants, which turn red in the summer, makes up the foreground; sometimes the scene is misty or foggy and other times it is

sparkling clear. The curvilinear line of the Little Sur River flowing into the Pacific Ocean is always photogenic. As you look across Highway 1 to the east, there are some dramatic sand dunes that turn brown in the late-afternoon light. One evening I was photographing them when a group of three coyotes walked across them right in front of me.

18.2 Miles: Point Sur Lighthouse (67)

Shortly after the Little Sur River, you will see the Point Sur Lighthouse, which became a state historic park in 1984. Several turnouts along Highway 1 provide nice views of Point Sur and the lighthouse. I prefer to take this shot in the morning when the sun lights up the foreground, the beach, and Point Sur, but I have also taken some nice shots in the evening

Point Sur Lighthouse in the fog

when the lighthouse silhouettes against the red sky at sunset. A little farther south at mile 18.8 is the main entrance and a road that goes to a parking lot at the base of the lighthouse. Lighthouse tours are available on the weekends; for more information, call 831-625-4419.

21.7 Miles: Andrew Molera State Park (68)

Andrew Molera State Park is about 7.5 square miles, making it the largest park along the Big Sur coast. Approximately 20 miles of hiking trails provide a variety of views from the beach to trails that are high in the hills. Also, the Big Sur River flows through the park, and the Beach Trail takes you to the river's estuary. Another spectacular hike is the Bluff Trail, which goes along a cliff above the Pacific. I do not have a favorite photograph in Andrew Molera; I prefer the hills across Highway 1, which are reached by driving up the Old Coast Road. From November to April these rolling hills turn a bright green and in March and April often have fields of California poppies. However, there is an excellent shot from Andrew Molera of Pico Blanco, the large pyramid-shaped mountain to the east. This vista is best in the afternoon when the sun lights up the face of the granite peak.

27.3 Miles: Pfeiffer Big Sur State Park—Pfeiffer Beach (69)

Pfeiffer Beach is a well-known destination for photographers. A small creek meanders across the sand, and two arches in the rocks light up when the sun shines through them at sunset. Unfortunately, finding the ideal window of time and the proper conditions to photograph these arches to get the optimal shot is not easy.

The arches light up best when the sun is farthest south on the horizon—closest to the winter solstice. But there is often haze or fog along the Big Sur coast, so the best conditions come after a late-day storm when the evening sky is clear and the sun is setting on the horizon. The final consideration: The arches photograph best at low tide. So prepare to photograph them from early December to mid January, after a storm, and around 4 to 6 p.m. when the tide is low and the sun is setting. When all of these conditions are in place, plan on arriving early because there will be five or six other photographers staking out their places with their tripods. Be assured, though, that this photograph is worth the effort that this planning and good luck involve.

Directions: The turnout to Pfeiffer Beach is not marked on Highway 1—even the official California State Parks Web site says it is hard to find!—so I recommend that you turn into the Big Sur visitors center or a local gas station and ask directions. However, once you turn onto the road to Pfeiffer Beach and drive about 100 yards, a sign on a large rock wall indicates that the beach is 2 miles away. Note that the road is narrow and winding and not recommended for campers or cars with trailers.

Turnout South of Big Sur (70)

About 5 miles south of Big Sur is a large, paved turnout on the ocean side of Highway 1 that has an excellent view to the south. Here you'll find a familiar image of the receding hills angling down into the Pacific. I cannot be more exact because there is no point at which Big Sur ends, but you should be able to find this large

McWay Fall at Julia Pfeiffer Burns State Park

vista. A picture of a whale has been painted on the pavement, but I am not sure how long this will last. It is a few miles north of Julia Pfeiffer Burns State Park.

I particularly like this view during the winter rainy season when there is a lot of moisture in the air and the hills fade into the mist. If you can't be there on a rainy day, try late afternoon or at sunset. It is important to let these hills fill the frame; be careful not to compose the picture so that they end in the center, which is a common mistake.

Julia Pfeiffer Burns State Park— Redwoods and McWay Falls (71)

McWay Creek flows through Julia Pfeiffer Burns State Park and forms waterfalls on both sides of Highway 1. The best-known, and most often photographed, waterfall is shown above. It spills about 100 feet onto the beach in a small cove on the ocean side of the highway. A tunnel under Highway 1 leads to the short pathway to the waterfall. This is a spectacular image due to the turquoise color of the water in the cove, the sandy beach, and the high rock bluff. The path becomes a wooden walkway that provides several vantage points for taking this image, and they are all good. Clouds in the background make the image even better. I have been there quite a few times, and the sky is usually clear, so I try to minimize it in the photograph. If you are driving on Highway 1, this is one stop you do not want do miss.

The other waterfall, which is on the east side of Highway 1, is located in the redwood forest in the main part of the park, just behind the picnic tables at the beginning of the Ewoldsen Trail. I have spent quite a bit of time exploring the trails in Julia Pfeiffer Burns and have found this to be a good location for photographing redwoods and McWay Creek within the redwood environment. Even on sunny days I can usually find some locations where the trees block the sun, which allows for much better photographs. I like to get down low and include something like a fern or large rock in the foreground, with the stream providing a counterpoint.

Tip: If you want to include rocks in the foreground of your creek photographs, they will look a lot better if you splash some water on them. Wet rocks are darker and more saturated in color than dry rocks. This is also a situation where you might want to use a polarizing filter to re-duce the glare and reflection off the wet rocks. A polarizer will also allow you to "see" into the water and include some underwater elements, such as rocks, on the streambed.

Gamboa Point Vista for Big Creek Bridge (72)

A half mile south of Big Creek Bridge is a paved turnout on the Pacific side of Highway 1 called Gamboa Point. This is a good location to photograph the Big Sur coastline to the north with Big Creek Bridge in the background. The area east of the bridge and along Big Creek is a large reserve that is part of the University of California Natural Reserve System and is controlled by the University of Santa Cruz. This wilderness area is used for research and contains a wide variety of

South Coast of Big Sur with pampas grass

plant and animal life including several endangered species.

Another viewpoint of Big Creek Bridge, which I also like, is at a gravel turnout about 1 mile farther south—marked by an old cement pad at the entrance. Looking to the north, Gamboa Beach is in the foreground, identified by five palm trees that were planted in a row, next to the bluffs at the back of the beach. From this far away Big Creek Bridge is much smaller, but the view of the coastline is very dramatic. As with all coastline photographs, the best time to shoot is late afternoon, when the light is more horizontal and has a warmer tone.

Tip: When you shoot north along the coastline, you are usually perpendicular to the sun, so try using a polarizing filter to see if you like the effect it gives. A polarizer will bring out the clouds and saturate the colors.

Lime Kiln State Park (73)

I probably drove by Lime Kiln State Park a couple of dozen times before I decided to stop and explore it. Lime was shipped out of this canyon for a short time in the 1870s, and one trail leads to the old kilns that are interesting to look at even though they are not particularly good subjects for photography. But another trail leads to a striking waterfall, and this is worth the hike for the photographs. Unfortunately, this waterfall is in the sun during most of the day, so you have to arrive early or late or be lucky enough to visit on a cloudy day. The trail to the waterfall is closed during the rainy season, when the bridges are temporarily removed for high water. If your timing is right, however, this beautiful waterfall is well worth the short (0.5

mile) hike to its base. The beach with many large rocks also looks interesting, but I have not yet had the time to photograph it.

Lime Kiln Canyon is one of the steepest along the Big Sur coastline. It rises over 5,000 feet to the well-known Cone Peak in less than 3 miles, which explains the waterfall. Cone Peak is often covered with snow in the winter.

Nacimiento Fergusson Road (74)

Just south of Lucia on Highway 1, Nacimiento Fergusson Road heads east and climbs up the coastal range before winding its way to Highway 101 near King City. Before the bridges were built on Highway 1, the old settlers used to walk east along roads like this one for their supplies. These trips could take several days each way and no doubt always provided adventure. Now Nacimiento Fergusson Road crosses Hunter Liggett, a military base that is actively in use for rugged-terrain training and is currently off limits for photography. The road also passes very near the San Antonio Mission and a beautiful old hunting lodge designed by Julia Morgan, the same architect who designed Hearst Castle and several buildings at Asilomar Conference Grounds in Monterey. If you are driving across this road to Highway 101, the mission is a very worthwhile stop. Although photography is not allowed inside Hunter Liggett, it is allowed at the San Antonio Mission.

As you drive up Nacimiento Fergusson Road, there are excellent views of the Big Sur coastline both to the north and south. Looking south, you can see Highway 1 winding along the coastline, and this makes a dramatic photograph in a variety

View from Nacimiento Fergusson Road

of lighting situations. One of my favorites was taken on a stormy winter day when the road disappeared into the mist. I also like the shot of the coastline to the north with the rolling hills in the foreground. I could give you the exact mileage to the turnouts I use, but I think you will enjoy discovering your own. You do not have to drive very far before the views become apparent.

Salmon Creek Falls (75)

I have stopped to photograph Salmon Creek Falls on at least two occasions and have been frustrated each time because I cannot find a good view or a good position to photograph it from. The short hike to the bottom of the falls becomes more difficult as you approach the falls,

and large boulders at its base block the view. Also, it picks up a lot of sunlight, which creates harsh, contrasty images. If you are driving by, though, you might want to stop, have a look, and decide if you want to take the trail to try to get a good image. There is a small turnout off Highway 1 to the north of the falls.

Ragged Point from Turnout (76)

A large rest stop just north of Ragged Point includes a restaurant, a gas station, and a motel, and I always am happy to stop over. If you walk to the back of the property, there are nice gardens and a pleasant path that leads to a bluff high above the ocean. While I cannot recommend this as a place to find many photographs, I can recommend it as a pleasant stop for lunch or just to take a break from the curves of Highway 1.

Ragged Point is just south of here, and there is a large turnout. It is interesting to look at, although I have never been there at a good time for photography, which would be at sunset or sunrise or on a stormy day with interesting cloud formations.

San Carpoforo Creek (77)

I am sure that I have driven past this little creek many times and not noticed it. But in the winter the banks of the creek are filled with colorful wildflowers, and it does make a strong photograph. It is located just south of Ragged Point, and Highway 1 curves inward quite a bit since there is not a large bridge. When you drive this section of the highway, stop and have a look, and see if you like this little creek as much as I did.

Piedras Blancas—Elephant Seals (78)

Just south of Piedras Blancas Lighthouse, a very large colony of elephant seals comes ashore every winter to give birth and mate again. The growth of this colony is an interesting story. The first elephant seals were spotted about 1990, at which time only a couple dozen came ashore and formed a small group. I remember first seeing it in the mid 1990s. The colony has grown at a staggering rate, and is currently estimated to be well over 10,000 and still growing! The seals now stretch along the beach for many miles, and there is a well-marked vista point with walkways and docents to answer questions and watch out for the safety of both the animals and their human visitors. I think that the elephant seals at Piedras Blancas are much easier to photo-

graph than those at Año Nuevo because you can get much closer, plus as you go along the walkway, you can have your choice of groups or large males as the subjects of your photographs. I used my 80–400mm VR lens on a tripod, which was perfect for zooming in on individual seals or backing off and getting small group shots. As with any wildlife, it takes a lot of patience and time to get strong images, but this is one stop along Highway 1 that is well worth the effort

For more information on the elephant seals at Piedras Blancas you can call

Salmon Creek Fall

Friends of the Elephant Seal at 805-924-1628, or visit their Web site at www.elephantseal.org.

Tip: I have found that to get good wildlife images, you have to shoot a lot and be very patient. I always feel like the first 15 minutes or so are just "warming up" as I become more aware of the animals and their behavior. In this type of situation it is really beneficial to be able to shoot with a digital camera—you can delete images in the camera, take a lot of pictures, and make ISO adjustments as you go along. Don't forget to use your flash!

Old Schoolhouse with Hearst Castle—San Simeon (79)

Across from Hearst Castle a turnoff to the right goes to the small "town" of San Simeon. A pier was built there by William Randolph Hearst, from where he exported local products such as grain, hides, and tallow. He also established a general store that is well worth a visit because it has not changed very much since it opened in 1873. Looking back to the east is the old schoolhouse, which sits alone in the middle of a field with Hearst Castle on a hill in the background. I think it makes an interesting photograph in late afternoon or evening, especially in the winter or spring when the grass is green and flowers are blooming.

Hearst Castle (80)

Hearst Castle, or *La Cuesta Encantada* ("The Enchanted Hill"), is surely one of the largest attractions along the central California coast. The architectural designs of this lavish estate were a collaborative effort between Julia Morgan, a pioneering female architect, and William Randolph Hearst. It is set high in the rolling hills of the Santa Lucia Mountains in the center of the 86,000-acre Hearst Ranch. Hearst Castle was well known in the early 20th century as a gathering place for the Hollywood elite, politicians, and prominent businessmen of the day. It was (and is) a showplace for Hearst's very large European art collection.

Hearst Castle offers four basic tours that visit various sections of the estate and a couple of more unusual tours, such as the sunset tour, on weekends. All the tours include the famous Neptune's Pool, the Greco-Roman outdoor pool, and the stunning Roman Pool, which is lined with gold and Venetian glass. I think these pools are the most photogenic part of the tours, along with the beautiful rolling green hills that surround the castle. In the wintertime it is possible to just show up and take the tours, but in the summer they are sold out in advance, so it is important to make a reservation: 800-444-4445 or 805-927-4621. There is also a Web site, www.hearstcastle.com. The new films they show on the tours are very well done.

Old schoolhouse at San Simeon

Santa Rosa Creek

Pico Beach (81)

Pico Beach is located just north of San Simeon State Beach, and there are many good photographic choices along this dramatic stretch of coastline. A stairway leads down to a sandy beach area, but I have photographed the large rocks in the Pacific from the bluff above the beach at sunset. As with many sunset and beach shots along the California coastline, so much depends on the quality and character of the sunset. If there are clouds on the horizon and the sun can go under them and illuminate them, the image can be outstanding. But even mediocre sunsets can still bring a lot of color and depth to the sky. I have learned not to try to guess what the sunset is going to be like but just show up and see if it develops.

Santa Rosa Creek in Cambria (82)

Santa Rosa Creek is at the southern end of Moonstone Beach Drive, which turns off of Highway 1 just north of Cambria. As you make your way south along this drive, there are many motels and small resorts—great places to stay because they are located just across the street from the ocean. You can leave your room for an afternoon or morning walk along the beach and look for locations to return for photography at sunrise and sunset. I like Santa Rosa Creek, and found several angles to shoot it from as it flows into the Pacific. This creek has a nice S curve, and interesting pieces of driftwood can be positioned in the foreground of the image. This beach area is my favorite part of Cambria.

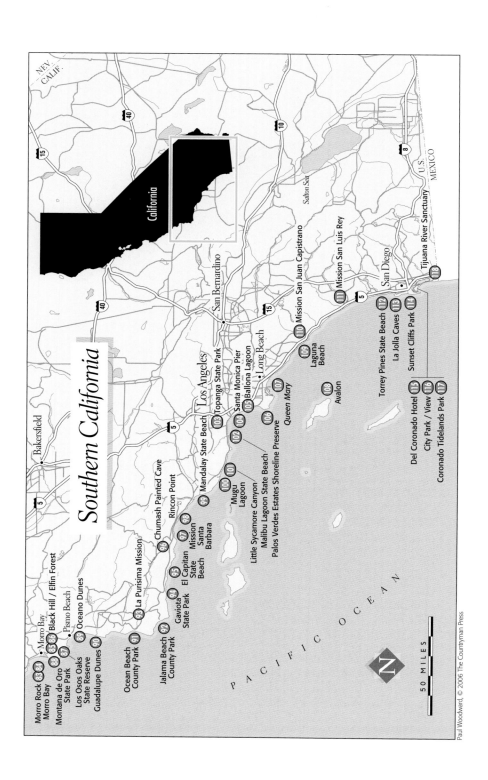

Southern California

California
NEV.
CALIF.

Bakersfield

San Bernardino

Los Angeles

Santa Barbara

Long Beach

Salton Sea

Mission San Juan Capistrano

Mission San Luis Rey

San Diego

U.S.
MEXICO

PACIFIC OCEAN

Morro Rock 83 84
Morro Bay • Morro Bay
Montana de Oro 85 86 • Black Hill / Elfin Forest
State Park 87 • Pismo Beach
Los Osos Oaks 88 Oceano Dunes
State Reserve 89
Guadalupe Dunes 90

Ocean Beach 91
County Park

Jalama Beach 92
County Park

Gaviota 93
State Park
El Capitan 94
State
Beach 95

La Purisima Mission

Chumash Painted Cave 96
Rincon Point 97
Mission 98
Santa Barbara
Mandalay State Beach 99

Mugu 100
Lagoon 101
Little Sycamore Canyon
Malibu Lagoon State Beach 102
Palos Verdes Estates Shoreline Preserve 103
Topanga State Park
Santa Monica Pier 104
Ballona Lagoon 105 106
Queen Mary 107

Avalon 108

Laguna 109
Beach

110

111

Torrey Pines State Beach 112
La Jolla Caves 113
Sunset Cliffs Park 114

Del Coronado Hotel 115
City Park / View 116
Coronado Tidelands Park 117

Tijuana River Sanctuary 118

N

50 MILES

Paul Woodward, © 2006 The Countryman Press

Southern California— Morro Rock to Mexico

Morro Rock from Embarcadero Road (83)

This is one of my favorite locations for photographing Morro Rock. As you drive along the waterfront and piers in Morro Bay, continue north to Embarcadero Road instead of turning left onto the causeway to Morro Rock. This road soon becomes gravel and heads into a beach area. As you enter this area, follow the road to the left, back to the ocean, and soon Morro Rock will appear with small, rolling sand dunes in the foreground. There are many places to park, and as you walk around, you will find nice spots to set up your tripod, with dunes and grasses in the foreground and Morro Rock in the background. I like this area early in the morning as the sun is just rising from the east and creating a soft sidelight on both the grasses and Morro Rock. I have not been there at sunset but imagine it would also be good at that time.

Morro Rock is composed of dacite, an igneous rock that is the remnant of a very old volcanic intrusion that did not totally form. The old volcanic ash and sedimentary dirt has been washed or blown away over the millions of years leaving only the core rock formation. Morro Rock was an island until 1938, when the causeway was filled in and completed. As an island it was a navigational aid to the Spanish ships that sailed up and down the California coast for several centuries. As you drive out to the end of the causeway, you can park and hopefully locate the pair of

Morro Rock from Embarcadero Road

peregrine falcons nest high up on the rock face. There are usually bird-watchers with spotting scopes observing and photographing the falcons, which are more visible in late April to May as they come lower to teach their fledglings to fly. I put a 400mm lens on my digital camera and got a pretty clear shot of a small falcon high up in a nest, but a longer lens would be better.

Morro Bay Harbor with Fishing Boats (84)

I always enjoy walking along the waterfront in Morro Bay and photographing the fishing boats tied up at the docks. Morro Bay is still one of the most important fishing areas along the California coast, and the weather-worn boats have a lot of appeal. I also look for coiled up fishing nets, which can be very colorful and make interesting "local-color" compositions. I prefer to photograph these boats either early in the morning or late in the afternoon with a sidelight instead of an overhead light. I have not been in Morro Bay on a foggy day but am certain that these conditions would also be very interesting for photographing the boats.

I have not taken the boat ride out to the sand spit that separates Morro Bay from the Pacific, but I am sure that there would be some interesting photo opportunities and unusual perspectives of Morro Rock from across the bay. The "clam taxi" departs from the Morro Bay marina on Embarcadero Road.

Morro Rock from Black Hill (85)

You may have seen this view of Morro Rock on calendars or postcards and wondered where it was taken from. At first glance it appears as though there are no hills behind Morro Bay from where you could get this perspective of Morro Rock with the town in the foreground. I will try to give careful directions since this hill is a bit tricky to find. Black Hill is just south of Highway 1 in Morro Bay State Park. If you are in the town of Morro Bay, follow Main Street into the state park. As you enter the park, there is a golf course, and as you drive past the clubhouse, take the left turn. This does not look like a road, and it feels as though you are driving into the golf course (which you are), but continue past the golf course, and this becomes Upper State Park Road. It is 0.7 mile up the hill to a small parking lot at the base of Black Hill Overlook. There is signage once you reach the parking lot, which is also the end of the road. The overlook is about a 10- to 15-minute uphill walk on a trail that eventually leads to a striking view of Morro Rock—the second of my three favorites.

Again, the best time to be at the overlook is at sunrise or sunset. I have seen very strong images taken just as the sun has set, there is still light in the sky, and lights are showing along the dock. There are times that the view is totally obscured by fog, so be sure to check the conditions before you make the effort to climb to the top of the hill. Good luck. The view is worth the hike!

Elfin Forest in Los Osos (86)

As you leave Morro Bay and continue south to Los Osos, I recommend that you visit the Elfin Forest. This 90-acre preserve was formed by the Small Wilderness Area Preservation (SWAP) located in Los Osos, and the name "Elfin Forest" comes from the stunted California live oaks that grow there. Although these oaks can be centuries old, they are only about 12 feet tall instead of the normal 50 feet elsewhere in the state. This area reminds me of the pygmy forests located farther north in and around Mendocino.

The Elfin Forest is my third favorite location for photographing Morro Rock. As you enter the forest, follow the raised boardwalk, which forms a loop, to two viewpoints: Bush Lupine Point and Siena's View. My favorite is Siena's View, but you should check both. The interesting thing about this perspective of Morro Rock is that the estuary, Morro Bay, is in the foreground, and at low tide there is very little water. The formations left by the receding water are small sand dunes, which can catch the light and create a strong texture or set of leading lines taking you into the image. Morro Rock is in the distance, so you may want to use a small telephoto, such as a 200mm, to bring it closer. These overlooks are also good locations for photographing the egrets and herons that inhabit the estuary. I have also taken some photographs of the stunted oaks but find that it is hard to make them look small without a point of reference. If you have the time, the short walk around the loop is well worth it. Be sure to pick up a trail guide at one of the entrances.

Directions: As you head south out of Morro Bay, take Bay Boulevard, and turn right (west) at the stoplight onto Santa Ysabel. As you drive along Santa Ysabel, there are several residential streets that you can turn onto to park and enter the forest; I recommend 12th or 13th Streets. For more information, go to www.elfin forest.org.

Los Osos Oaks State Reserve (87)

This is a very old grove of California live oaks, and the trees are well developed, with limbs that grow at unusual angles,

which make for very interesting photographs. Some of the oaks are also dwarfed, as they are in the Elfin Forest, due to the lack of nutrients in the soil. A trail winds its way through the oaks, and as you walk along, you will find many interesting perspectives for your images. Avoid this park when the sun is out because the images will have too much contrast. I recommend a visit when it is foggy or early or late in the day.

Directions: Los Osos Oaks State Reserve is located on the south side of Los Osos Valley Road, just east of the intersection with Bay Boulevard. Look for a small turnout parking lot with signage.

Montana de Oro State Park (88)

This park is called "Mountain of Gold" due to the orange California poppies and yellow wild mustard that cover the large Valencia Peak in the spring. But don't

Creek in Montana de Oro State Park

worry if you are not in the park during March and April; there are many other things to photograph. I particularly like the small coves located along the shoreline. The volcanic rock formations and Monterey shales, which are common in this park, provide interesting diagonal, uplifted rock strata that are often covered with a green moss or algae near the ocean. The contorted and uplifted rock strata always make me wish I had studied more geology!

Directions: Montana de Oro State Park is located along the coast just south of Los Osos and Morro Bay. Follow Los Osos Valley Road west until it turns into Pecho Valley Road and turns south along the coastline. There is signage for the entrance to the large park area.

Oceano Dunes at Pismo State Beach (89)

If you have never visited the Oceano Dunes area, you are in for a surprise and an exciting visual experience. These dunes have been famously photographed by Ansel Adams, and this is also the location where Edward Weston photographed many of his nudes of Charis Wilson. I think these dunes are as interesting and dramatic as those in Death Valley, especially in late afternoon, when the horizontal sunlight creates dark shadows in the windblown surface of the sand.

Tip: Many hiking trails traverse these dunes, and they are off limits to off-road vehicles. Be careful that you do not put footprints in the dunes that you will later want to photograph. My best images were

Oceano Dunes

taken looking north in late afternoon. I was looking for the dark and interesting shadows formed by the horizontal light. Sunset is too late because you need the sunlight to create the shadows. I have not photographed this area early in the morning but assume that the shadows would be formed then, as well. These sand dune shots look best when shot with a wide-angle lens, and I used an 81A filter for most of them. I was very pleased with the images I took from my visit and highly recommend this area.

Directions: The dunes area is located south of Pismo Beach and west of Oceano along the Pacific Ocean. From Highway 1, 2 miles south of Pismo Beach, follow the signs that lead you to the entrance of Pismo State Beach. After paying the park admission at the tollbooth, drive onto the beach, and turn south on the hard-packed sand. You do not need a four-wheel-drive vehicle; many trailers are towed to various campgrounds on the beach! Go about 1 mile until you drive across the Arroyo Grande Creek; just below the creek and slightly inland are the vegetation-free high dunes. There may be other interesting areas in these dunes to photograph, but this is the location that I most enjoyed. For more information about Pismo State Beach, call 805-489-2684.

Rancho Guadalupe–Nipomo Dunes Preserve (90)

As you drive south leaving Pismo Beach, Highway 1 and Highway 101 diverge, and both go inland from the coastline. Several interesting and somewhat remote beach areas lie between Pismo Beach and Santa Barbara. The first of these is Rancho Guadalupe–Nipomo Dunes Pre-

serve, just south of the mouth of the Santa Maria River and west of the small town of Guadalupe. If you hike south along the beach, you will eventually come to the 450-foot-high Mussel Rock, the highest sand dune on the West Coast. The view to the north is spectacular: You can see for several miles as the ocean meets the unobstructed shoreline. There are some restrictions about where you can walk on the dunes since this is a nesting area for the snowy plover, but there are many open and available areas.

Directions: From Highway 1, turn west on Main Street, and follow the road to the Nipomo Dunes Preserve, now under the protection of The Nature Conservancy.

Ocean Beach County Park (91)

Ocean Beach County Park is an isolated beach at the mouth of the Santa Ynez River. The park encompasses 36 acres and a portion of the lagoon. It is completely surrounded by Vandenberg Air Force Base, which allows about 5 miles of beach to be open to the public. There is an old railroad platform that dates from 1897. The lagoon and the grasses that grow in the dunes offer many opportunities for interesting photographs, although portions of the beach are closed from March through September to protect the nesting snowy plover, a threatened species.

Directions: From Highway 1, turn west on Ocean Park Road (Highway 246), about 15 miles west of Lompoc, and follow the road for 10 miles.

Jalama Beach County Park (92)

Jalama Beach County Park is the best-known of the isolated beaches between Pismo Beach and Santa Barbara, probably because it is a surfing destination. Jalama Beach Road winds for about 15 miles south and west of Highway 1, crossing Jalama Creek several times before arriving at the beach. Once there, you will find a campground and the well-known Jalama Beach Store and Grill, a fun place to have lunch and watch the surfers. Jalama Creek is located just north of Point Conception, where the California coastline turns inland to the east. There are opportunities for interesting photographs along the road as you approach the beach and along Jalama Creek as it enters the ocean. This is a fairly remote beach area, so be sure you allow sufficient time to drive to the beach and explore for photographic possibilities. On the cliffs above the beach are the tracks for the Amtrak Coast Starlite, which may provide the best views of this remote coastline since it follows the beach through remote areas where there are no roads or trails. For more information about Jalama Beach Park, call 805-736-3504.

La Purisima Mission State Historic Park (93)

Between Santa Barbara and Pismo Beach, Highway 1 turns inland, away from the beach. Just east of Lompoc is the La Purisima Mission, which I think is one of the most interesting of the California missions. As with most of the California missions, La Purisima fell on hard times in the early part of the 19th century. Diseases introduced by the Spanish decimated the native Indian population, and during the Mexican Revolution the mission was commandeered by soldiers, who demanded support. Eventually the mission was sold to private landowners by the Mexican government and fell into total disrepair. Then in the 1930s, under Roosevelt's New Deal, the Civilian Conservation Corps rebuilt the mission on its original foundations. This project took seven years, and many of the workers learned the required skills on the job. The result is a beautifully restored mission that has the primitive character and feeling that it probably had several centuries ago. But there is also a lot of sensitivity in the painted walls in the chapels, which reminded me of similar places I have observed in Mexico. I highly recommend a visit to this mission if you are in the area. I particularly enjoyed photographing the restored rooms with their artifacts and the chapel with its subtle colorations and simple altars.

Gaviota State Park (94)

Gaviota State Park is located west of Santa Barbara, just south of the intersection of Highway 1 and Highway 101. The park includes about 5 miles of shoreline and the mouth of Gaviota Creek, which forms a deep gorge running north to south into the ocean. There is also a pier built in 1874, where local goods were loaded onto schooners. Since this beach faces south instead of west, the morning and afternoon light provide an interesting cross-lighting effect that is different, and in some ways more interesting, than photographing into the sunset.

As I have mentioned previously, I always enjoy photographing small creeks as they cut through the sand and flow into the ocean. Such creeks as Gaviota Creek provide leading lines and add a lot of interest to photographs of beach areas. I also found a strong image just outside the park, where the hills were covered with yellow mustard flowers. I was fortunate to be

Mustard flowers near Gaviota State Park

there on an overcast day in the spring, and after walking around, I discovered a location where I could include some dark, dead tree branches in the foreground, as shown above.

El Capitan State Beach (95)

At this state beach, a small, rocky creek, El Capitan Creek, flows into the ocean, and provides an interesting area to photograph. Follow the Nature Walk along the creek as it winds through large sycamores, and look for photographs of the spreading tree branches. As you follow the walk to the ocean, there are very interesting large, moss-covered rocks. I spent quite a bit of time photographing these rocks, which are much better without direct sunlight on them. Even without the direct sunlight, I

found that a polarizing filter helped reduce the blue of the sky and enhance the dark green of the moss. I enjoyed this beach area a lot and highly recommend it. This area has ringtail cats, and we think we caught a fleeting glimpse of one.

Directions: El Capitan State Beach is located about 15 miles east of Gaviota State Park and about 15 miles west of Santa Barbara, just off of Highway 101. The entrance to the park is well marked from the highway.

Chumash Cave Paintings (96)

I always seek out Indian petroglyphs and pictographs, and these are some of the best I have seen, so I highly recommend this location. Unfortunately, these colorful paintings are behind a locked gate and

The famed Mission Santa Barbara

somewhat difficult to photograph, but I was able to get some surprisingly good images. There are a couple of openings in the gate, and I leaned my camera on a tripod so that the lens went through the lower opening, and I used a flash on an extension cord through the upper opening. It is dark inside the cave, so I suggest that you bring a strong flashlight to shine on the paintings to focus your camera. The next time I am in the area I will contact the state parks office to see if I can get one of the rangers to give me access inside the cave; perhaps you can do likewise. For a preview of the paintings, go to www.sb nature.org/research/anthro/chumash/pcart.htm.

Directions: Drive north on San Marcos Pass Road (Highway 154) for several miles. The first road to the right is Paint-ed Cave Road. Follow this small, winding road for 2 miles, and the Painted Cave is on the left. This road is too narrow for large campers or trailers, and there are only a few parking places on the side of the road when you reach the cave.

Mission Santa Barbara (97)

No trip to Santa Barbara is complete without a visit to the large and beautiful neoclassical Santa Barbara Mission. The mission was originally founded in 1786 and has been continuously occupied by the Franciscans since that time. It features a façade made of sandstone blocks and twin bell towers, a design borrowed from an old temple that existed in pre-Christian Rome. There were actually three adobe churches here, each larger than the other, the last destroyed by an earthquake in 1812. The present church was finished and dedicated in 1820. It sustained extensive damage during the earthquake of 1925 but was restored by 1927.

Other than the front façade, my favorite area to photograph is the arcade, with its multiple arches that run along the front of the building. I like the perspective of the receding columns, especially when the light is soft. Along this corridor are colorful doorways and interesting benches, which also make very good subjects for photography. Plus there is a very nice fountain in the front of the mission. I framed a photograph with the fountain on the right and the mission on the left and used a two-stop neutral-density filter to darken the mission and bring out more detail in the darker fountain. Since there are so many visitors to the mission, and people walk in and out of your photographs,

I suggest arriving early in the morning before the tour buses unload.

Directions: From Highway 101, take Mission Street exit east approximately 0.75 mile; then go left on Laguna Street. The mission is at 2201 Laguna Street.

Rincon Point (98)

Rincon Point is one of the best-known surfing locations in central California, if not the entire state. Follow the path from the parking lot, and you will be close enough to the surfers to be able to take great photographs. Because this area is so good and accessible, other photographers are often on the beach. I walked along the rocky shoreline about 100 yards to get even closer to the larger waves and better surfers and have some very good images.

Surfing at Rincon Point

Of course, this location is best on an overcast day or late in the afternoon, but I think it is well worth a visit anytime you are in the area. I set up with a heavy tripod and used a 400mm lens on my digital body, so I was able to fill the frames with the surfers. Even if you do not have a long lens, Rincon Point is still a good place to both photograph and watch some very good surfers in action.

Directions: Rincon Point is located off of Highway 101, just as you cross the Ventura County line. A turnoff at Bates Road is just south of the gated community at Rincon. From the large parking lot (with rest rooms) it is a short walk down to the beach.

Mandalay State Beach (99)

I like walking through and photographing in this undeveloped area because of the grasses and patterns in the sand created by the afternoon winds. I use a very wide-angle lens such as a 20mm and get down low to place the grasses or textures in the sand in the foreground and the waves and clouds in the background. Another way to photograph these dunes is to set your camera higher and photograph the dunes as a pattern. These dunes are pretty high, and it makes an interesting shot to have them recede into the background. Since this beach faces west, the best times to visit and photograph are early morning or late afternoon, unless you are lucky enough to be there on a stormy day.

Directions: As you drive south on Highway 101, take the turnoff onto Harbor Boulevard just north of Ventura Harbor. Harbor Boulevard follows the coastline south through Ventura and Oxnard and is a much more pleasant and scenic road

than 101. About 1 to 2 miles south of the Santa Clara River, turn right, or west, onto Fifth Street, and follow it to Mandalay Beach Road. Mandalay State Beach will be on your right—a small, undeveloped beach area just north of the many houses being built along Mandalay Beach Road.

Mugu Lagoon (100)

Although Mugu Lagoon is one of the largest salt marshes in California, attracting thousands of migrating birds, including endangered California least terns and Belding's savannah sparrows, this 1,800-acre lagoon is entirely located within the U.S. Navy's Pacific Missile Test Center and is off limits to the public. But all is not lost. It is possible to arrange group tours in advance to see the birds by calling the Navy Public Affairs Office at 805-989-8094. The Mugu Lagoon was the site of several Chumash Indian settlements, including some villages that are 7,000 years old. In fact, the best artifacts from the Chumash culture were found in the lagoon area.

There is a public vista point off of Highway 1, where it is possible to see the lagoon and perhaps some birds close at hand. The vista point is located just south of the naval station and is clearly marked from the highway. There is also Point Mugu Beach and State Park, a couple of miles farther south along Highway 1. The last time I was there, the entrance into the park was blocked off and the park closed due to winter rains and landslides. If you are in this area during the summer or fall months, the road should be open, and there could be a lot of migrating birds.

I did take some satisfying photographs along the road just south of Point Mugu

One of the wild parrots living in Little Sycamore Canyon

Beach. There are nice grasses growing along the highway, and I found some interesting rock formations on the beach below, all of which I combined into one photograph. Be cautious when photographing along Highway 1 because the local traffic moves very quickly, and the road is narrow.

Little Sycamore Canyon (101)

Little Sycamore Canyon is located about 3 miles southeast of Mugu Lagoon on the east side of Highway 1. There is a nice campground and a stream to walk along that flows from the hills above into Sycamore Cove. But for me the most interesting thing in Sycamore Canyon is the group of bright green wild parrots living there, as shown above. They are fed by the park rangers, and sometimes it is possible to get very close to them, making for great images. You can hear them as you drive into the park, and their clatter made

me think I was in a tropical rainforest. The parrots make Little Sycamore Canyon well worth the visit since it is so unusual to see them in the wild.

There are many more interesting beach areas along this lovely stretch of Highway 1 as you drive east to Malibu. I always enjoy this section of the road and highly recommend it.

Malibu Lagoon State Beach (102)

I found the most interesting part of the Malibu Lagoon State Beach was the Adamson House, located next to the state beach on Malibu Creek. This 1929 Spanish-style house was designed by the well-known architect Stiles Clements and built for Merritt Huntley Adamson and his wife, Rhoda. Adamson was an attorney and later a very successful dairy farmer. He started the Adohr Stock Farms—"Adohr" is Rhoda spelled backward—and became a very large milk producer.

Fountain at the Adamson House, Malibu Lagoon State Beach

This house is well known for the colorful Malibu tiles that decorate it both inside and out. No two tiles are the same, and they present numerous photographic opportunities. I particularly liked the fountain areas at the back and side of the house. The Adamson House is a museum and a State Historical Landmark, and tours can be arranged by calling 213-456-9497.

Topanga State Park (103)

Hiking in the 9,000-acre Topanga State Park can make you forget that you are in or near Los Angeles with its overcrowded freeways and acres of concrete. As you drive up Topanga Canyon Boulevard, which runs north off of Highway 1, head for the parking lot next to the ranger station at Trippet Ranch. A short, 1.5-mile trail winds through Santa Ynez Canyon and leads to a striking 20-foot-high water-

fall. This waterfall is my favorite location in Topanga Canyon, and in the winter and the spring many wildflowers, including tiger lilies and orchids, grow around the fall. Other hiking trails in Topanga include some that go high into the hills and give wide, sweeping views of the Pacific Ocean below. The park is a refuge for wildlife, and it is always possible to come across deer, bobcats, foxes, and a variety of snakes and lizards.

Santa Monica Municipal Pier (104)

I am including the Santa Monica Pier because I like the way it looks from the sidewalk that goes along the beach or from the beach itself. But I have always been frustrated by the photographs I have taken of it. I think I have been too close—maybe a better location would be from farther away, with a telephoto lens instead of a wide angle. Perhaps you can be more successful in finding a good vantage point. The next time I go, I will try to photograph it from the south instead of the north where I have had several unsuccessful attempts.

The pier is one location where I do not feel that I can be very helpful, except to say that I like the way it looks at dusk when the lights start to come on and there is still color in the sky. I should warn you that it is also a difficult location to get to because of the way Highway 1 merges into the city traffic just south of the pier. I recommend that you just try to get close, park your car, and walk.

Ballona Lagoon and Wetlands and Marina del Rey (105)

The Ballona Wetlands are a good example of a wetlands area that has been almost totally erased by development. Originally the wetlands covered more than 1,700 acres and provided drainage for the Los Angeles River; today, the wetlands have been reduced to a few hundred acres. However, these few hundred acres still provide an important environment for both migratory birds and the many that live there year-round. It is possible to photograph herons and cranes in the wetlands and at some areas of the Ballona Creek. My favorite location is a bed & breakfast in Playa del Rey called the Inn at Playa del Rey (telephone 310-574-1920). Several of their rooms and a deck offer good sites for viewing birds in the lagoon. Unfortunately, the lagoon is fenced, so it is not possible to enter it without going on an organized trip. There are, however, a few raised walkways and platforms that are available at all times and allow you to get closer to the wildlife. Also from this inn it is possible to walk around Del Rey

Lagoon Park and along the edge of Marina del Rey Harbor, one of the largest manmade harbors in the world. This is a pleasant part of Los Angeles and also provides opportunities to photograph the harbor area and the many private boats.

Malaga Cove and Palos Verdes Estates Shoreline Preserve (106)

I am sure there are many interesting locations to photograph along the shoreline in the city of Los Angeles, but I have to admit that the huge volume of traffic and the difficulty of going anywhere and then parking has discouraged me from exploring and enjoying this area. But south of Los Angeles on the Palos Verdes Peninsula, in a community more residential and easier to navigate, I enjoy the Palos Verdes Shoreline Preserve. As you drive along the peninsula south of Malaga Cove, many small and steep trails lead down to the rocky shoreline and very interesting rock formations below the bluffs. As with almost all western seaside shots, the best time to photograph is at sunset or on cloudy days. Be careful walking down these steep trails, especially if they are wet and slippery.

Queen Mary in Long Beach (107)

The *Queen Mary* is a former British luxury liner that made many trans-Atlantic voyages between 1934 and 1964, until it was decommissioned and moored permanently in Long Beach Harbor, at the end of the 710 Freeway, just south of Long Beach. It is now a hotel with shops and restaurants. Next to the *Queen Mary* is a Russian submarine that is open for tours. These are both tourist attractions and fun to visit if you are in the area, particularly with children.

The Queen Mary *in Long Beach*

There are some unique photo opportunities to be had here, particularly if you enjoy taking pictures of large and dramatic machines. It is possible to get close to the bow of the *Queen Mary* and exaggerate the size with a wide-angle lens. I took the photograph above from the other side of the ship when I took the ferry to Catalina Island, which departs just a short distance from where the *Queen Mary* is moored.

Catalina Island and Avalon (108)

Catalina Island is well worth the visit if you have the time. Ferries to Catalina leave from several locations—including San Pedro, Long Beach, Newport, and, in the summer months, Marina del Rey—and arrive in the small, charming town of Avalon, which has quite a few hotels and sidewalk restaurants. The trip takes about one hour and is very pleasant when the weather is good. It is easy to go over to Catalina Island in the morning and return the same afternoon, but I suggest a longer visit since there is a lot to see on the island. Catalina, which is about 75 square miles, has been inhabited for at least 7,000 years and has over 2,000 archeological sites.

There are many great hiking trails that take you into the hilly interior, but most are restricted. Many of the trails are controlled by the Catalina Island Conservancy and require a permit. These permits are readily available, even on the day of your hike, at the conservancy office, which is located at 125 Chelsea Avenue—just a short walk up from the main street that goes along the waterfront. I found office staff to be very helpful and they also have good trail maps. (You can get more information about the conservancy and about hiking on Catalina through www.catalina conservancy.org or calling 310-510-2595. Even more information about hiking on the island is available by calling the Los Angeles County Department of Parks and Recreation at 213-510-0688.)

Catalina is also well known for snorkeling and scuba diving because it is located at the meeting of the cool California current and the warmer southern California countercurrent, which allows for a large diversity in sea life near the island.

I suggest that you be ready with your camera as the ferry approaches the island; I always like the views of Avalon with the harbor and boats in the foreground. You can also take this shot as you are leaving the island. In the evening you can get a very nice overview and photographs of Avalon by walking up the hill behind the ferry landing. I like this shot just as the lights of the city are coming up and there is still color in the sky. It is also a good image when there is a full moon. You will need a tripod and a medium-sized to long lens for this shot.

City of Laguna Beach (109)

Laguna Beach is well known as an artist's enclave along the southern California coast and there are many interesting shops and galleries in this small city. I always enjoy my visits to Laguna Beach. Main Beach—at the intersection of Laguna Canyon Road (Broadway) and the Pacific Coast Highway (Highway 1)—is always crowded with swimmers and surfers and is great if you enjoy photographing people and activities such as volleyball or surfing. I also like the Aliso Beach County Park, which is located a couple miles south

Avalon on Catalina Island

along the Pacific Coast Highway. A small creek flows into the Pacific here during the winter and provides interesting photo opportunities in the evening or at sunset. This beach also attracts a lot of people, so I enjoy going there during winter storms when it is more deserted.

Mission San Juan Capistrano (110)

I enjoy visiting all the California missions, and I think that the Mission at San Juan Capistrano is one of the most interesting and photogenic. This mission is appealing because it was destroyed by an earthquake in 1812, and the large old church is now in ruins. The dark brown crumbling adobe walls make for very good photographs, but they make for even better photographs when there is no sunlight on them. Look for the bell tower with three old bells inside of arches and the beautiful fountain. The last time I was there was during Swallow Days, when the swallows return from South America to their home in the mission. During this weekend celebration the mission is full of activity and people, which is entertaining but presents difficult conditions for photography. For the best photo opportunities, I suggest avoiding holidays and special events and arriving early in the morning or late in the afternoon.

Directions: Mission San Juan Capistrano is located about 3 miles inland off Interstate 5, just north of Dana Point. The mission is open daily; for more information, call 714-493-1111.

Mission San Luis Rey (111)

As with all the old missions in California, Mission San Luis Rey—or Mission San Luis Rey de Francia—has had a turbulent and interesting history. It is often referred to as the King of the Missions because it is the largest and, in many ways, the best preserved. Mission San Luis Rey was one of the last California missions to be built—18th of the 21 missions—and was positioned between the already-existing San Diego and San Juan Capistrano Missions. Life at the mission began in 1798 and continued until secularization in 1833, at which time the Spanish Franciscans turned it over to the Mexican government. During the politically turbulent years of the Mexican-American War, Mission San Luis Rey, like most of the California missions, was sold into private hands. The missions were then used for a variety of purposes, including housing soldiers engaged in the conflict, and suffered a lot of deterioration. When the Mexican War ended and California became a state in 1850, President Lincoln returned this mission to the Catholic church. But it was not until the late 19th and early 20th centuries that this and other missions underwent major reconstruction and improvements. Now the Mission San Luis Rey is administered by the Franciscans and is a National Historic Landmark.

The Mission San Luis Rey is considered by many to be the most attractive of all the California missions. It has a striking yellow exterior and contains design elements from Spanish, Moorish, and Mexican styles of architecture.

Aside from taking photographs of the mission from the front, I found many other good photographs by walking through the museum area. There is a collection of santos (carved sculptures of saints) in the museum in acrylic cases. There are also reproductions of various rooms as they were in the last century, and these, too, make good images. Unfortu-

Mission at San Luis Rey

nately tripods are not allowed in the museum or mission interior area, so you will need either high-speed film or a higher ISO adjustment, such as 800, on a digital camera. For more information, call 760-757-3651 or visit www.sanluisrey.org.

Tip: When photographing through glass, be sure to photograph at an angle so that you do not reflect in the image.

Directions: From Interstate 5 take Highway 76 east for 4 miles, and turn left on Rancho Del Oro Road to the mission entrance.

Torrey Pines State Reserve, State Beach and Los Penasquitos Lagoon (112)

The Torrey pine is the world's rarest pine tree, found in only two locations: the Torrey Pines State Reserve and on Santa Rosa Island off the southern California coast. This thousand-acre park was originally purchased by Ellen Scripps in the early 1900s with the understanding that it would protect the environment for the Torrey pine and be available for public use. A charming old adobe lodge in the

Eroded sandstone formations at
La Jolla Caves

reserve is now the visitors center, with exhibits of local plants and animals. The many trails begin at this lodge and lead through the hills and down to the beach. I cannot recommend specific areas for photographs, but there are many opportunities for wildlife and birds, particularly down at the Los Penasquitos Lagoon, a salt-marsh area located just north of the Torrey Pines Reserve. If you can locate a pine tree with an interesting shape, they make nice silhouettes with a brightly colored sky at sunset.

Directions: These three locations are adjacent to and located just off of Torrey Pines Road, west of Interstate 5. The parks are well marked on the highway; driving south, take the Carmel Valley Road exit, and follow it west to Torrey Pines State Beach. The lagoon and reserve are located just to the south.

La Jolla Caves (113)

These eroded sandstone cliffs and caves are my favorite location for photography in southern California. At low tide the green moss and tide pools enhance the interesting shapes of the eroded, brownish sandstone. As with most coastal scenes, it is best to photograph the La Jolla Caves early or late or on a cloudy day. If there is a slight drizzle, the moisture will make the colors even more saturated. If you are able to visit this area, I recommend that you allow a lot of time because there is so much to photograph. The interesting rock formations remind me of those at Point Lobos. Be very careful when scrambling on the rocks as they can be very slippery and dangerous when wet.

Directions: The La Jolla Caves are located at the south end of La Jolla Bay,

Rocks at Sunset Cliffs

where Torrey Pines Road intersects Coast Boulevard.

Sunset Cliffs Park (114)

Sunset Cliffs Park is composed of 68 acres of bluffs, walking paths, and beach—albeit limited-access beach. Very interesting formations are located in the eroded sandstone bluffs that are enhanced with caves and green moss. The bluffs are also a good place to view migrating California gray whales during winter months or to bird-watch. There are several very large, round formations of rocks that I have not seen anywhere else, and these provide strong details or focal points for photographs. This area has the same sandstone formations as La Jolla Caves a little to the north, and both locations provide many opportunities for good photographs, especially at low tide on overcast days.

Tip: I found that I could emphasize the brown coloration on a cloudy day by adding an 81A filter. This filter also helps the green mossy areas on the rocks. In addition to the 81A, you might try a polarizer to eliminate some of the glare and emphasize the brown coloration of the rocks. Directions: From Interstate 5, go west on Freeway 8 until it becomes Sunset Cliffs Boulevard. Follow Sunset Cliffs Boulevard south about 1.5 miles to Sunset Cliffs Park. Once there, park and look for a trail that leads down to the bluffs.

Del Coronado Hotel (115)

A visit to San Diego would not be complete without stopping by the spectacular Del Coronado Hotel, the largest Victorian building in California and a National Historic Landmark. The Coronado Hotel was constructed in 1888 on what was viewed as a wild spit of land far removed from "civilization." In the early 20th century, the Coronado was well known internationally and was the first hotel west of the Mississippi to use electric lights. Over the years this striking hotel has opened its rooms to many famous guests, and now there is a Hall of History in the lower level with a mini museum that includes old guest lists. I like to walk around and photograph this hotel at dusk as the lights are coming up and there is still ambient light in the sky. If you walk into the back courtyard, behind the restaurant, there is a nice view of the cone-shaped tower that becomes redder in the evening when lights are shining on it.

Another good place to shoot is the San Diego–Coronado Bridge. Built in 1969 to replace the ferry service that served the hotel for many years, the bridge rises about 250 feet above the water to allow large ships to pass underneath. It makes a striking photograph, especially in the evening or on a misty, foggy day.

View of San Diego from City Park (116)

There is a very nice view of San Diego from Coronado Island in the city park that used to be the location of the ticket booth for the old ferry. This park is located on the corner of Orange and First Streets, and in the evening the lights of the buildings are reflected in the water of San Diego Bay.

Coronado Tidelands Park (117)

This park has a walkway that goes along the shoreline of San Diego Bay, offering several good locations for photographing the San Diego–Coronado Bridge. There are moored sailboats in the foreground,

which you can add to the photographs of the bridge to give a sense of proportion and depth.

Directions: As you drive over the San Diego–Coronado Bridge from San Diego to Coronado Island, this park is located just at the end of the bridge. Watch carefully for the right-hand turn.

Tijuana River National Estuarine Sanctuary and Border Field State Park (118)

The Tijuana River National Estuarine Sanctuary and the Border Field State Park are the southernmost parks along the California coastline and comprise southern California's largest and most diverse wetlands: 2,531 acres of tidal wetlands and the largest saltwater marsh in California. I think the best way to visit this area is to start at the visitors center, which is open 10 to 5, Wednesday through Sunday. From there you can access the McCoy Trail, which follows the marshy area both north and south. This is a great trail for taking photographs of a wide variety of birds, including a very large population of light-footed clapper rails. While I was there, I also took some good photographs of the hillsides covered in bright-yellow mustard flowers. Be aware, though, that helicopters frequently fly overhead— no doubt the border patrol on duty.

Directions: The visitors center is located just off of Interstate 5. Take exit 4, which is also Coronado Boulevard, and go west for about 2.5 miles. Then turn left on Third Street, and left again on Caspian Way, which becomes the parking lot. For more information, visit www.tijuana estuary.com.

A California condor in Big Sur, now back from the edge of extinction

Favorites

Favorite Towns and Small Cities
Trinidad
Mendocino
Gualala
Bolinas
Pacific Grove
Cambria
Morro Bay
Avalon (Catalina Island)
Malibu
Laguna Beach
Coronado

Favorite Wetlands
Arcata Marsh and Wildlife Sanctuary
Humboldt Bay—South Bay
Bodega Bay
Tomales Bay
Elkhorn Slough
Morro Bay

Favorite Beaches and Tide Pools
Luffenholtz Beach
Manchester State Beach
Salt Point State Park
Carmel River State Beach—Ribera Beach
Weston Beach at Point Lobos
Garrapata Beach
Pfeiffer Beach
La Jolla Caves

Favorite Harbors
Trinidad Bay
Monterey Bay
Morro Bay
Avalon Bay

Starfish at low tide at Point Lobos

Garrapata Creek Bridge

Favorite State Parks and Reserves

Western Union Landing State Beach
Van Damme State Park
Manchester State Beach
Año Nuevo State Park
Point Lobos State Reserve

Garrapata State Park
Pismo State Beach—Nipomo Dunes
Torrey Pines State Reserve

Favorite Lighthouses

Point Arena
Point Reyes
Pigeon Point
Point Pinos
Point Sur

Favorite Landmark Photographs

Point Arena Lighthouse
Pigeon Point Lighthouse
Golden Gate Bridge
Arch at Pfeiffer Beach
McWay Falls in Julia Pfeiffer Burns
    State Park
Morro Rock
Nipomo Dunes

Sunset at the Pigeon Point Lighthouse